Campus Shock

Campus Shock

A
FIRSTHAND REPORT
ON
COLLEGE LIFE TODAY

Lansing Lamont

E. P. DUTTON · NEW YORK

For information contact:
E. P. Dutton, 2 Park Avenue, New York, N.Y. 10016

Library of Congress Cataloging in Publication Data

Lamont, Lansing.
Campus shock.

Bibliography: p. 133
1. College students—United States.
2. Education, Higher—United States—1965–
I. Title.
LA229.L28 1979   378.73   79–608

ISBN: 0-525-07309-4

Published simultaneously in Canada by
Clarke, Irwin & Company Limited
Toronto and Vancouver

Designed by Abe Lerner

10 9 8 7 6 5 4 3 2 1

First Edition

for

DOUGLAS, LISA, VIRGINIA AND TOMMY

to whom we entrust

the future

THIS IS A REPORT on the dark side of college life in the 1970s. It is about that significant minority of students who were unable to cope with the relentless academic and social pressures of the decade. The findings in this report are neither scientific nor conclusive. They represent a journalist's impressions based on months of extensive reporting across the country. The case histories are true, though several of the scenarios are composites of various stories related to me. In a few cases names have been changed to protect a student's privacy.

Contents

Acknowledgments

THIS STORY is the distillation of 675 interviews with students, teachers, parents and administrators. I traveled to twelve select universities for my reportage and spent additional months researching past and current views of the campus scene from numerous articles, surveys and books, among them the notable works of David Riesman and Seymour Lipset and the excellent *Growing Up in America* by Fred and Grace Hechinger.

While the Bibliography acknowledges my debt to a large number of published sources, some of the statistics and quotations in the text are based on additional material that has appeared in leading publications, principally the *New York Times*, *Wall Street Journal*, *Washington Post*, *Time*, *Newsweek*, *Change* magazine and the *Chronicle of Higher Education*.

A number of university presidents gave generously of their time and thoughts to this project: Derek Bok of Harvard; William McGill of Columbia; Kingman Brewster and A. Bartlett Giamatti, former and current presidents of Yale; Richard Lyman of Stanford; Martin Meyerson of Pennsylvania; John Kemeny of Dartmouth; Robben Fleming of Michigan (now president of the Corporation for Public Broadcasting); William Bowen of Princeton and Alfred Bowker, chancellor of the University of California at Berkeley.

I am indebted, too, to several deans who provided me with particularly useful insights: Henry Coleman of Columbia; David Knapp, provost of Cornell; Fred Hargadon of Stanford; Lee Verstandig of Brown; Adele Simmons, formerly of Princeton (now president of Hampshire College); and Lorna Straus of the University of Chicago. Archie Epps and Charles Whitlock of Harvard were especially helpful.

It would be impossible to list all the faculty members and advisers who offered me their views, equally impossible to include all those chaplains, psychiatrists and social counselors who recounted for me in painful detail how the pressures had affected students and altered their values. But at bottom, theirs was the most brutally informing perspective on the ills of this generation. For that I am in their debt.

My thanks go also to those public affairs officers whose scheduling efforts on my behalf were herculean, notably James Merritt of Princeton, Robert Graham of Dartmouth, Bryant Robey of Cornell, Joel Berger of Michigan, Robert Beyers of Stanford, Martha Matzke of Brown, Raymond Colvig of Berkeley, Theodore Driesch of Pennsylvania and Stanley Flink of Yale.

Robert Lamb, a friend with a keen eye for the nuances of student behavior, provided me with helpful material and advice based on his teaching experiences at Columbia and the University of Pennsylvania.

For their thoughtful demands, above all for their patient assistance in seeing this manuscript through to print, I am grateful to Amy Clampitt, my editor, and to Jack Macrae, president of E. P. Dutton. To Rya Rosenzweig, I award the Order of the Sore Typing Finger, and to my wife, Ada, a bouquet of gratitude for spurring me on when the spirit flagged.

Finally, the students. It is foolhardy, if not presumptuous, for a writer to attempt to freeze in time the character and tides of a college generation. Their mood can be as ephemeral as last year's rock hits, change colors more swiftly than the seasons. But for better or worse, this generation at the elite schools remained constant throughout the decade in its fears, its yearnings and values. I think I've sifted some kernels of truth from all that the students told me of their experience. I wish I could credit each of them by name. They made this book possible.

L. L.

Campus Shock

I

The 1970s:
What Went Wrong?

On a January afternoon in 1976, Charles Blair, a University of Michigan senior, turned off the ignition switch in his Volkswagen camper and unsheathed his .12-gauge hunting shotgun. At that hour his parents were arriving in Ann Arbor to attend his graduation. In his feverish determination to graduate early that year and beat out the June rush for jobs, Blair had doubled his academic work load and spent the semester toiling through the nights to keep his marks above water. He had betrayed no hint of despondency when he phoned his parents a few days before; he'd already bought a cap and gown for the exercises, he told them. At the ceremony, the senior Blairs could not find their son. Students in the off-campus apartment house where he lived said he had gone to hunt ducks that morning. A week later his empty camper was found half buried under snowdrifts on a side road. His frozen body lay near by, the shotgun beside it. His family now learned that he had fallen so far behind in his studies that there was no chance of his graduating; he'd picked up his third failing grade only days before he shot himself. "But he couldn't bring himself to tell his parents," an official at the university explained. "The pressures were just too bad."

For most parents in the decade that is now ending, if their sons and daughters no longer appeared on the evening news screaming obscenities at the Establishment, it followed that they were secure and thriving in college. But the assumption was mistaken, the calm an illusion.

As a reporter returning home after five years abroad, I caught unmistakable signals from friends with college-age children that all was not right, that something was poisoning the life of undergraduates at the most prestigious universities, that many students were unhappy, beset by tension, trapped in insecurity and frustration.

To learn what the trouble was, I set out to explore a dozen preeminent liberal arts universities: the eight Ivy League schools of the East (Brown, Columbia, Cornell, Dartmouth, Harvard, Pennsylvania, Princeton and Yale); and farther west, the state universities of Michigan at Ann Arbor and California at Berkeley, as well as Stanford and the University of Chicago, both private institutions.

Though hardly inclusive, this group of universities seemed to represent the best in higher education. Historically, they had produced a majority of the leaders in public and professional life. The experience that is shaping the one hundred thousand or so students now enrolled at these schools can thus be expected to have telling consequences for the character of American leadership by the year 2000. What I found persuaded me that a documentary on the troubled students of this decade, one that would bury the comforting myth of tranquillity on the campus, was called for.

It could be said that if the 1960s had resembled in some respects a media-orchestrated protest revel, the 1970s were a decade of quiet but no less real revolution among students—a revolution of new social experiences, aspirations and responses to pressure. The inner turmoil experienced by these young people would seem to have been unprecedented. At no time before have the once-sheltered elite universities been subjected to pressures so numerous or so complex: racial, sexual, economic and environmental as well as academic.

Those pressures came during a decade of recovery and transition at the universities, and to many students like Charles Blair —a fictitious name for an actual case—they seemed in the end unendurable. Students were assailed by doubts over whether their heavy financial investment and tireless study would pay off in the tightening market for jobs and for places in graduate school. Social forces beyond their control brought changes in racial and sexual relationships as more blacks and women enrolled. There were restrictions on their privacy and their once casual life style, imposed by overcrowding and the threat of violent crime. The competition for grades was savage, the anxiety acute. A neurotic dread of failure, such as led to the suicide of Charles Blair, afflicted growing numbers of college students all through the 1970s.

As a result of all this, students besieged campus psychiatric clinics. Hundreds dropped out of college for a semester, a year, sometimes for good. A despondent graduate student at Brown, and another at Dartmouth, became the first suicide statistics at those schools in a decade; a score of Cornellians, mostly undergraduates, had killed themselves in the last ten years. A chaplain at Princeton described the mood among students as "an epidemic of despair." Vandalism and abusive drinking increased, as did outbreaks of cheating and sabotage. At a number of colleges, the honor system disintegrated. In the fiercely competitive atmosphere many students came to regard one another less as colleagues than as adversaries in a survival course.

They fought each other—sometimes physically—not only for grades, jobs and coveted graduate school positions, but for financial aid, choice housing, even the books on reserve in the overused libraries. "You understand that everybody is your enemy," wrote a young Harvard M.B.A., "and you learn to fear and hate people, to live in crowded isolation." Many students withdrew into a self-imposed monasticism, shunning friends and advisers. A dean at one Ivy League college told of undergraduates closeting themselves in their rooms for days, drunk or listlessly incommunicado.

Among a sizable minority of students, the obsession with grades, with accreditation, with achievement at all cost, signified a generation that had come close to losing its soul to the demons of competitive stress. It had given rise to doubts about whether the brightest of these young people would mature into anything more than ultrasmart lawyers and overpaid medical whizzes.

Despite all this, and despite the importance of the great universities to our society, the past few years have given us a largely one-dimensional view of what goes on inside them. Journalistic reporting on education is often restricted to bloodless accounts of curricular change or academic controversy. These are important matters, but they tell little of the human struggle that is the heart of the learning process. Without an insight into the personal traumas of college life, above all among students, we tend to harbor the illusion that pain and corruption stop outside the campus gate—that the universities, relieved of yesterday's political turmoil, have returned to being custodians of all things rational and serene. Precisely because we make such assumptions about their influence on our young, an unsparing look at what actually goes on behind their walls is all the more necessary. What is to be found there raises the disturbing question: will the current crop of graduates, for all their undeniable talent, enrich or impoverish our future?

2

Lost Civility

In the winter of 1976, a plaintive message appeared on lamp-posts around the campus at Cornell:

Disgusted with the pressures? The dehumanization? If so, you're not alone. We're people before students, who must relate to the world and to each other. You may want to join us. Call Alice at 256–5572 for one person's explanation of a desperate attempt to make Cornell a real place to live.

"Alice" was the pseudonym that Elizabeth Harrison, a 19-year-old sophomore from the New York City borough of Queens, had adopted to protect herself from the derisive calls she half expected. But there were none. In less than a week, forty-five other lonely and alienated students responded to her laboriously typed and stenciled notice, and Elizabeth was making plans for a party to bring them all together in her tacky off-campus residence. It had taken a year and a half of her college life to reach out for the human connection she craved, and in the end she was driven to advertising for it.

Fully a third of undergraduates surveyed at Cornell around the same time had complained of loneliness. Authorities at Princeton who toured the dormitories during one academic term in the late 1970s discovered that students living along the same corridor hadn't even met. Ivy League officials deplored the increasing difficulty of keeping track of students—some on leave of absence or moving to off-campus rooms, others surreptitiously leaving assigned quarters to move in with friends of the oppo-

site sex. On a March day in her junior year, recalled Kathy
Holub, Harvard '76, "a roommate whom I'd dimly perceived at
the edge of my life materialized next to me, cradling me in her
arms while I screamed out my fear, my anger and loneliness."

"They don't give a damn about us," declared Paul Ryder, a
senior at the University of Michigan. "They don't care about
the quality of our life." The same complaint, in different words,
was being aired on other campuses, where students felt ignored
or short-changed in their expectations. "The brochures give you
the idea you'll be having lunch with Daniel Patrick Moynihan,"
said a sophomore at Harvard. "In the end, if you're able to land
a course with a famous professor, it will be in a lecture hall
filled with six hundred students. You might as well watch him
on TV."

Of Harvard undergraduates who in a 1974 survey were asked
about their expectations of the university, 58 percent checked
"the chance to learn from great teachers." In retrospect, however, only 17 percent of that number reported that their expectations had been fulfilled.

The inability of even the most prestigious institutions to
provide students with fulfilling lives either within or outside the
classroom was an outgrowth of a quarter century of expansion
that had reached its apogee a decade before. In the words of
Robben Fleming, president of the University of Michigan, "We
paid the price. We lost some of the old human dimensions."
What he meant is suggested by a look at that university's
housing troubles: since 1968 its enrollment had risen by some
4,000 students, yet no new housing for single students had been
built and more than two-thirds of the students were forced to
live off campus after their freshman year, many of them paying
exorbitant rents for squalid quarters. By the middle of the
1970s, crowding and competitiveness had made the once con-
vivial residential houses at schools like Harvard distinguish-
able from apartment hotels, according to one observer, only by
the friendliness of the kitchen help. The comfortable if snob-
bish intimacy of the elite schools had been replaced by a new
egalitarianism. There was greater diversity in the student body,
but many undergraduates found it harder to discover those
around them with like interests.

The era of specialized studies increased the sense of isolation. Professors immersed themselves in their scholarly arcana, premeds studied and shop-talked among themselves, minority students clustered within their own camp. Administrators appeared ever more distant and impervious; college presidents had become in many instances almost like wraiths. With few exceptions, most had forsaken their academic disciplines to become crisis managers; presidents such as Fleming of Michigan, a former arbiter of labor disputes, were chosen more for their skill as mediators (and fund-raisers). A few retained a certain dash and feel for the concerns of students, but others seemed to disappear into the paneling of their offices, the victims of bureaucratization and too many hours spent huddling with lawyers.

The gulf between student and teacher continued to widen as professors discovered fewer visible rewards for their instructional prowess than for their publishing fecundity. There were no Nobel prizes in undergraduate education, and those who staked their careers on teaching had little to show for it outside their classes. (That splendid dinosaur from the age of the caring, dedicated teacher, Charles Townsend Copeland of Harvard, had to wait eighteen years before the school's scholarship-obsessed faculty promoted him to assistant professor.) During the 1960s, many older professors, dismayed by the violence of the student protest movement, had retreated still further into scholarship; in the 1970s, younger, untenured faculty members, their promotions and job security threatened by economic retrenchment, scrambled to shore up their scholarly credentials, reducing their teaching and counseling commitments wherever possible. Graduate instructors and teaching assistants shut their doors on students to concentrate on their own problems. A Harvard freshman in difficulty finally called it quits after his faculty adviser, over a period of several months, failed for the fifth time in a row to keep an appointment.

Cynically, some students had come to identify a whole category of professors as opportunists for whom teaching was little more than a vehicle for ego-tripping, for personal glory. "The last thing I want to do is go back to Harvard and teach undergraduates," Henry Kissinger told a journalist before he left the State Department. Judith Hambleton, a senior at Brown, complained: "My psychology professor spends his time teaching a course that's limited to *his* research work. I can't reach him to ask questions, he has no office hours. When he's finished his lecture, he picks up his notes, runs off the podium and disappears to the hospital where he works." Another Ivy League junior concluded, "The students here who need individual attention the least are almost the only ones who get it."

At a time when more students than ever required the testimony of their teachers to be accepted for graduate work, the aloofness of some professors could destroy their chances: a bright but shy senior who'd been enrolled mostly in large lecture courses might be denied admission because no professor knew him or her well enough to write a letter of recommendation.

The decline in the quality of life could not be blamed entirely on university administrations and faculties, however. On many a campus, *civitas*, what the educator Daniel Bell called the spontaneous willingness to respect the rights of others, came perilously close to dissolving.

Students went to unheard-of lengths to thwart their competitors—a Columbia premed reset his classmates' alarm clocks so that they'd oversleep and miss a critical exam—and there were reports of increasingly frequent temper outbursts in the dorms. The case of Stewart Todd, a freshman at Michigan, was all too typical. Nightly his efforts at concentration were shattered by the blare of acid rock from his roommate's stereo. The roommate ignored all pleas for quiet; the dormitory proctor declined to intervene. After several weeks of this, Todd's test scores and equilibrium both crumbled. One night there was a scuffle, during which Todd kicked in one of the offending speakers. Then, with six stitches for a split lip, he found a peace of sorts in the infirmary.

Nor was the plight of Sylvia Webb, a junior at Princeton, by any means an isolated one. On the first night that her roommate had brought a man up to their dormitory quarters, she had retreated to the bathroom to finish studying for a math exam. When she emerged at 2 A.M. the man was still there, and within a week he'd become a regular overnight guest. Gradually,

Webb's privacy was preempted. On nights when the library was overcrowded, she cadged an hour or two of uninterrupted study in a friend's room down the hall. Often she took along a sleeping bag and spent the night there on the floor, a refugee in her own dorm. As her study regimen fell apart, her doe eyes became ringed with fatigue, she cried easily, and some days she could barely stay awake in class.

Sharing and cooperation, two basic components of friendship, seemed no longer to be encouraged on college campuses. In 1978, Brown University's new president Howard Swearer devoted a special address to students on the need to rebuild community relations and a responsible dormitory life; an article in Dartmouth's undergraduate newspaper bemoaned the disappearance of the "humanist element of life" at the college. "There's a kind of anarchy going on," said Shelley Marks, another student at Michigan. "The authorities are afraid to impose rules, and the students seem unwilling to police themselves."

There was much to feed the churlishness of students as they languished in registration lines or dining-hall queues, struggled with the fine print in housing contracts, or vainly tried to persuade economy-minded administrations to restore hot breakfasts in the residential halls. The constant din moved one harried Princeton senior to recommend fines for those students who every night poured out of the campus pub and milled around shouting at each other. Even the libraries weren't spared. Crowding and lax enforcement of rules turned many of them into noisy combat zones, where a student was lucky either to find a seat in the evening or to lay hands on assigned reading materials. At the University of Chicago's Regenstein Library, students were seen wearing SPQR buttons—"Save Peace and Quiet at Regenstein."

The dormitories, once the civil bedrock of campus society, had themselves become a source of alienation. In the days when colleges functioned as surrogate parents, the now discredited parietal rules, however authoritarian, had made for a relatively benign atmosphere in the dorms. Once that authority had been removed, it was hard to find responsible faculty members who were willing to take charge of residential halls; the title of housemaster was regarded in some quarters as no more than a euphemism for zookeeper. In the new high-rise, cement-block buildings put up to house students as economically as possible, there was so little of either charm or comfort that, as one undergraduate put it, "People stop thinking they actually *live* here." By the same token, at schools such as Columbia, where the older residential halls were rundown and fire-prone, students complained of cockroaches and larger vermin, as well as of frequent lack of heat.

Increasingly, college buildings became the targets of vandals. A University of Chicago sophomore, Daphne Macklin, spoke almost with a shrug of seeing people "do in a whole lounge, kicking in glass doors and walls." Between September and December 1977, an official at Brown discovered 162 instances of vandalized fire extinguishers—some emptied, others broken, missing or destroyed; university police who responded to a fire that did serious damage to one college hall found two out of the building's four extinguishers empty. At Yale, a group of students smeared excrement and foul-smelling acid around the dining hall of their residential college. Cornell undergraduates took to wrecking the vending machines in their dorms. "Every morning I read the police report here on vandalism and it makes me sick," said a vice president of the university.

William Beall, chief of police at the University of California at Berkeley, declared that by the mid-1970s more damage had been inflicted inside the school's residence halls than during the entire riotous decade of the 1960s.

Much of the destruction was attributed to the increasingly abusive drinking, which by the middle of the decade had become the biggest drug problem on campuses. Students imbibed less for pleasure than for a release from the pressures. "They drink and get in brawls or they drink themselves so senseless they have to be hospitalized overnight," remarked Jim Lyons, the security director at Brown where in recent years authorities had initiated special programs and appointed a new dean to deal with the problem. Drugs, by comparison, though still in ample supply on campuses, were no longer deified; not only had the price in many cases become prohibitive; the memory of friends who'd blown their minds on bad acid or pot in the 1960s dissuaded many more students now who felt the need to stay in shape because of the competition for grades.

Indeed, the once scornfully regarded "grind" had become re-spectable. *pressure* At the same time, as the academic year became more compressed and the pace of study accelerated, there was less and less time for students to nurture new friendships or to examine their values and instruction. At Yale, where freshmen had once lingered to converse over coffee at wine-and-candle-light dinners in the residential colleges, there was no lingering now, but a stampede for the library before the tables were cleared. A sophomore at Berkeley, who dared to question a professor's interpretation in class, was booed by her classmates. They seemed to have been telling her, she reflected later, "Stop interrupting our education and let's get on with it!"

Drop Outs

There were many who, succumbing to the stress, dropped out of college for a semester, for a year, or permanently. Inter-rupting the traditional rhythms of sustained study and friend-ships, dropping out had become a salient trend of the decade—one that further depersonalized the atmosphere in the colleges, which many students had already come to view as little more than stepping stones to a career.

Across the country, half of those entering college never grad-uated. In the elite schools the dropouts ranged from frustrated minority students to the middle-class white children of bankers, brokers, Washington columnists and members of the President's cabinet. Along with battle fatigue, the reasons they gave for leaving included the need for self-discovery. "I wanted to learn to breathe and take things in around me," explained a Brown junior who left the campus for a semester.

Before 1968 the number of Harvard undergraduates on leave during a given year seldom exceeded 150; by the mid-1970s, ac-cording to a senior dean, as many as 770 were "out there in the bushes." The comings and goings of such students made it harder than before to project accurately the number who would be on hand at the start of an academic year. Massive overenroll-ments resulted and by the middle of the decade overcrowding had become an unacceptable norm. Cost-conscious universities, like airlines, preferred to overbook rather than risk having space unused.

At Yale, an error in computing the expected vacancies led to the enrollment of more than a hundred students above the number who could be accommodated. In the fall of 1977 Brown University found itself with 115 students too many. As housing arrangements collapsed in confusion, students were forced to double up or be housed in hastily converted lounges or storerooms, even in the infirmary. Many could anticipate spending their entire college lives shoehorned into dormitory suites designed for half the number of actual occupants. Undergraduates took crash courses in carpentry so they could erect plywood partitions in their packed suites to screen out roommates and preserve some semblance of privacy. Others, moonlighting as salesmen for space-saving loft beds, found themselves swamped with orders from classmates.

Early in 1978, incensed Columbia students forced the authorities to back down after they had proposed doubling up in two already overcrowded dorms. At Harvard, seniors in one house voted to withhold payment of gifts they'd pledged to the college alumni fund until the administration took steps to relieve the crowding. Meanwhile, at the University of Michigan, students who had been literally crowded out of the dorms posted offers of fifty-dollar rewards for anyone finding them a decent place to live off campus. The annual lottery to determine which upperclassmen and -women would be allowed to remain in the dorms had become a traumatic ritual, the losers departing frequently in tears to seek lodgings in Ann Arbor, where they might have to pay $250 a month for a two-bedroom apartment with peeling paint and a broken toilet. One sophomore who moved into an off-campus house during the winter had to endure faulty insulation and an explosion in a sewage pipe that deposited two feet of excrement in the basement.

Although the dropout craze had fueled the overload in the dorms, the root cause was the reluctance of the schools to construct newer residential halls during a decade when they had markedly increased their enrollments to attract extra revenue and to accommodate women at previously all-male institutions.

At Yale in the late 1960s, while the enrollment was increasing by nearly 30 percent, the number of student rooms had not been added to. By 1975 the residential colleges were filled to capacity and the undergraduate *Daily News* warned that the jam was creating a tension "that visibly alters student life." A woman junior complained of sharing a dormitory room "so small that two of us couldn't undress at the same time." Nearly one-fifth of all Yale upperclassmen were now living off the campus.

It was a situation that inevitably exposed more and more students to a new menace. Those living off campus on the fringes of urban ghettos like South Chicago, Harlem or New Haven knew the feeling; even *on* the campuses it caused a tightening in the gut. None were immune to a development whose effect could without exaggeration be described as revolutionary: the fear of violent crime.

3

Crime at the Gates

Snapshots of his puckish grin still remained to haunt the walls of the apartment that he had shared with his two Yale roommates about a mile east of the campus in New Haven. On a December night in 1974, Gary Stein had left that apartment to visit his girl, who lived not far away. On a quiet residential street, he was accosted by half-a-dozen teenagers who demanded money. When he appeared slow in producing his wallet, one of the youths pulled out a sawed-off shotgun and fired. The blast tore through Stein's stomach and the youths fled, leaving him dying on the sidewalk. It was the first killing of an undergraduate in Yale's 275-year history. With the murder of Gary Stein, much of that university's patrician innocence about the ghetto world at its doorstep died, too.

Yale in the 1970s had become an enclave of privilege in a city whose black ghetto had grown increasingly explosive. By the late 1960s, the university police had had to add a detective division to cope with the drug addicts who seemed to be everywhere. Security in the antiquated residential colleges amounted to a sieve: any bathroom, cubbyhole, steam tunnel or catwalk might conceal a prowler, and the old panels on doors to students' rooms could be pried off with the twist of a can opener. Some students' rooms were broken into as many as four times during a term. Strangers walked freely in and out of the dormitories at all hours, unchallenged by the cheerily nonchalant students who manned the security desks. In the newly permissive era it was not uncommon to find a group of young men and women outside their dorm in the wee hours of a spring morning, playing volleyball in the nude.

The shooting of Gary Stein destroyed overnight what remained of the aura of untouchability among Yale students. After a freshwoman was raped in her dormitory the first week of the 1975 fall term, the atmosphere worsened. A counselor described the "paranoia" among the women in her dorm as unbelievable. Another rape in a dormitory was reported a few months later; then a medical student was beaten and raped in a garage near the campus, and another woman was robbed and threatened with rape in her campus quarters. Yale now began to wall itself in.

Locks were placed on all campus buildings and gates, on dormitory entryways, on the doors to suites and bathrooms. Extra street lights and sidewalk emergency phones were installed, and a late-night shuttle bus service was revved up. Peepholes studded the doors of dormitory rooms; shrubbery behind which an intruder might lurk was removed from along the paths. Yale's forty-four-man police unit shed its low profile and donned uniforms for the first time. Its officers were outfitted with blackjacks and snubnosed .38 revolvers, and were ordered to report for regular target practice at the New Haven police academy. The university recruited students to help patrol the parking lots at night, issued special new identification cards and emblazoned the campus with posters warning students of the need for safety precautions.

In all, Yale spent nearly $100,000 to beef up its security. When it was through, the number of reported crimes had begun to diminish substantially. But so, too, had the spontaneity in students' lives.

At other elite universities, the story was much the same.

Bucolic Stanford was the scene of four homicides in less than two years, during 1973 and 1974. One of the victims was found in the campus church with a gouging knife wound in her head; another, a male physics student, was stabbed to death near the undergraduate library; two other women were strangled, one of them at a spot in the foothills behind the campus where she had set up her easel. Packs of teenagers sometimes ran through the campus at Berkeley, threatening students with knives or guns. More than 1,500 criminal incidents were reported on the campus in 1976, inciting the undergraduate newspaper to demand that the school take effective crime prevention steps as its first priority; at the same time, students living off the campus waged an urgent campaign to force their landlords to put bolt locks on all doors. Robberies at the university in the spring of 1978 had risen sharply.

In February of that year, a young English professor at Yale was stabbed as she walked down a path near the campus. Two months later at Columbia, a 25-year-old graduate student was cornered in her dormitory room by a fellow student who hurled a beaker of acid in her face, badly burning both eyes. Harvard freshmen were set upon by local toughs inside their own Yard, and just outside its gates the sophomore son of a U. S. Attorney General was so savaged by hoodlums that doctors had to operate from inside his mouth to repair the wounds. Of the nearly two hundred serious crimes reported on the Harvard campus during one year in the mid-1970s, 128 involved robbery and assault.

Some college authorities believed that far more assaults on women were occurring than had been reported—"I was hesitant to say I'd been raped," recalled a University of Chicago teacher who had been forcibly sodomized in her campus apartment—but the known figures on rape were alarming enough. For the first time, a woman reported being attacked inside one of Harvard's classic residential houses by the river; at least one freshwoman told of waking up in the dark to find an intruder in her dormitory bed. At the University of Pennsylvania, where authorities now log about a hundred obscene calls to students each year, two women were raped in the same science building in 1977, and early in 1978 there was another rape in a high-rise dormitory. During the first five months of 1978, the total number of rapes in the two Philadelphia precincts of which Penn is a part came to thirty-eight.

In the city of Berkeley, where during the mid-1970s a rape occurred on the average of every three days, the number of such assaults on the University of California campus by 1976 had gone up to seven in a year. In December 1975, the rape of a young woman in the stairwell of a campus residence hall had been followed just three days later by a fatal assault that took place on the campus. The victim was an attractive senior, Lucille Towers, who after an evening art class had taken a shortcut along a dimly lit path through a grove of eucalyptus trees bordering the stream known as Strawberry Creek. A campus policeman heard her screams, found the rapist methodically battering her head with a rock, and shot him. The girl lingered a week in a hospital and then died. Later, a classmate told a visitor that two other women had been attacked on that same path—"but a woman had to be murdered before the university responded and had the area properly lit."

Even daylight offered no guarantee of protection: two Stanford women were rushed by a knife-wielder as they strolled one afternoon in a crowded campus park and a 26-year-old graduate student was raped at knife-point while walking along a main avenue during the lunch hour.

On other campuses, there were complaints of insensitivity on the issue. "There's a bigger problem here than anyone imagines," said Eunice Burns, a women's organizer at the University of Michigan, where it was not unusual for undergraduates to be mugged while walking to class or molested in their dormitory washrooms and library carrels. "Everything's hushed up and consequently many women don't appreciate the danger. Men don't understand the problem, don't feel it in their gut like us, and men run this university."

Officials at the University of Michigan were worried, at any rate. "Crime runs high and runs bad here," one of them admitted. Of eleven rapes reported in Ann Arbor over the winter holiday season of 1976, four involved Michigan students. Ann Arbor, with a population of 50,000, had seen the number of reported crimes between 1965 and 1970 go up by 287 percent; and in 1974, the more than 10,000 individual crimes reported were equal to the number in Syracuse, New York, which has four times as many people. During the same five-year span, crimes in Cambridge, with a population of 100,000, had gone up by 113 percent, and in New Haven (population 140,000) by 210 percent.

Of the University of Chicago, whose Gothic-style towers are bounded by Lake Michigan on the east and elsewhere by crumbling black ghettos, a former student declared, "You don't live there long before a friend is raped or robbed." The statistics on crime for the police district that encompasses the university suggested, in fact, hardly less than a garrison under siege. In 1975, for example, the figures included 1,165 robberies, 458 assaults and 86 rapes. One of the student victims was the friend of a prelaw major, Tom Hessler. She was sitting in her car one day, waiting to pick Hessler up after class, when two men forced open the door and drove off with her. She was found hours after the rape, her clothes torn, her face purple with bruises. "She carries the scars, but psychologically I got hit the worst," Hessler declared.

After two undergraduates at Chicago had been held up and shot to death, the university added sixty-five officers to its police force (now one of the state's largest) and initiated a cross-campus bus service so students wouldn't have to negotiate the terrain on foot after dark. It installed more than a hundred white emergency telephones around the campus and even supplied the students with silver whistles to blow in case of attack. The accouterments of police security remained highly visible: armed officers stationed in major buildings, patrol cars purring along every other elm-lined street. But there were those who believed it would be years, if ever, before the fear dissipated. As the school bought up dilapidated buildings that abutted the campus, then demolished them, they left a kind of no-man's-land or cordon sanitaire in their place, heightening the students' sense of isolation. Many students felt almost trapped, afraid to venture off the campus because, as a chaplain said, "They think they're taking their lives in their hands."

Although at most universities the actual number of crimes remained small in proportion to the populace, the effect of an isolated killing or assault on the collective psyche was an acute and widespread anxiety. Many students found academic concentration difficult as their lives became enmeshed in a web of security regulations. Evening exam schedules had to be arranged so that students could be finished before dark; on some campuses, classes in karate became an informal part of the curriculum.

It had been a simpler matter to guard against thieves and rapists in the days when the sexes were segregated and campus police could deter any male found wandering after hours near a girls' dormitory. But tidal changes—the encroaching city slums, the drift of outsiders onto the campus that had begun during the antiwar protests, and the growth of a crime wave thought to be the worst since just after the Civil War—had caught the colleges unprepared. Their relatively small security forces had been trained to cope with sophomore drunks and panty raids, not with professional criminals. In the 1970s, with parietal rules dead and colleges generally more accessible to the public, criminals found the situation tailor-made for their purposes.

Thefts mainly accounted for the dramatic rise in campus crime statistics. At Harvard over a two-year stretch, the reported thefts went up from 730 with a total value of $96,000 to 1,280 worth $193,000. During the 1974 fall term, when estimates of the value of property stolen averaged between $3,000 and $4,000 each week, Harvard police announced that they would arrest any unauthorized person found in a campus building. The university and individual students at Michigan were being robbed altogether of property valued at from $200,000 to $250,000 a year. Bicycles were stolen in such numbers—hundreds of them disappearing on a single campus in the course of a year—that some universities stopped including them in their statistics. "We can't do much more unless we put bars on the windows," said a disgusted Yale official.

Although outsiders were responsible for most of the thievery, some officials believed there was more internal theft than ever on campus. David Gorski, a former security chief at Harvard, estimated that between 20 and 40 percent of thefts in residential houses there had been committed by undergraduates. The University of Pennsylvania's public safety director asserted that there was no way to account for so heavy a volume of thefts in the dormitories other than to assume that in most cases students were stealing from each other. Not many years back, observed Barbara Kauber, Cornell's judicial administrator, a student might promiscuously borrow an item or two—a book or a record. "Now, he'll steal not one item but a whole range of goods. It's no longer impulse stealing, either, but carefully planned."

One undergraduate at Cornell broke into an office shared by twenty graduate students and took every book in sight. On other campuses, students were known to have methodically rifled the entire wardrobe of a roommate. Wallets were lifted boldly not only from students' knapsacks and desks but from their jackets inside the classroom. Small furniture, telephones and wall paintings regularly vanished from common rooms; large quantities of silverware and glasses disappeared from dining halls. A sign over the cash register in Stanford's main cafeteria pleaded: "Bring back our dishware from your car, home or dorm. We lose $200 worth of dishes a week." Among $5,278 worth of property reported stolen at Berkeley one winter month in 1978 were a computer terminal, a laboratory telescope, a number of sculptures from the law school and several road barriers, all belonging to the university. Sophisticated student thieves sometimes misappropriated meal-ticket books and computerized billing cards that enabled them to eat free of charge for a year.

Motives for the thievery ranged from simple greed to a belief that for an individual to appropriate communal property was entirely legitimate. The "rip-off" psychology of some students imitated the shoplifting and short-changing that had become increasingly common among middle-class parents; it reflected a society so depersonalized that the belongings of others were no longer thought of as personal either. Still other student kleptos offered the creaky rationale that they were retaliating against a system that had been ripping *them* off.

Much of the pilferage centered on university bookstores, which many students regarded as natural enemies—establishment enterprises where prices often seemed extortionate. "They'll take whatever they want, a dollar-fifty paperback or a twenty-five-dollar art volume, it's indiscriminate," said one harried clerk. In the 1970s, stores on the campuses of some elite schools suffered annual losses from theft equal to between three and four percent of their gross earnings. At Berkeley, the figure reached $150,000 a year on a $2.5 million sales volume; then the store, like others, hired a plainclothes security staff and began turning student shoplifters over to the police instead of to tut-tutting deans.

The more discriminating book thieves, however, many of them affluent middle-class students, concentrated on works with a high resale value. They capitalized on their knowledge of which textbooks would be in greatest demand for a term course, as well as which ones were about to be dropped by the professor as required texts. The market thrived as inflation drove up book prices. Some student rings operated with near-professional panache, purloining books from fellow students and peddling them back to the book stores, or heisting volumes from the store shelves to sell at cut-rate prices to the students. As long as the price was right, no risk seemed too great: one student haul included a forty-five-dollar tome that weighed six and a half pounds.

At Columbia, officials at the university book store collared as many as five thieves a day, most of them students. "I get paranoid about it," confided one of the store's managers, who said he spent half his time trying to thwart such larcenous stratagems as peeling the "used" book labels from second-hand books and reaffixing them to new books in order to acquire the latter at bargain prices. "You can't stop it. You look them dead in the eye and they still rob you."

At every university where the main entrance to a residence hall now featured guards and inch-thick plexiglass doors, where a student had to decipher a coded lock or grope for an invisibly numbered I.D. card before being admitted to his or her own dorm, and where a simple visit to friends across campus entailed a tedious security check, the fortress atmosphere threatened to stifle casual relationships. Still more painfully invidious was the distrust it injected into the already tenuous relations between black and white students—thereby placing one more obstacle in the way of minority youths trying to make their way in the frequently alien world of the upper-crust white university.

4

Racial Distrust

The experience of Derrick Scott, a black student at the University of Michigan, was symptomatic. On his way to visit a friend living off campus, he had found himself hopelessly lost in a tidy neighborhood inhabited by middle-class whites. After twice attempting to ask directions of strangers who rushed past without answering, he rang a doorbell. The occupants of the brightly lit house peered out at him, then bolted the front door and closed the blinds.

For Scott, a bright and articulate achiever from the ghettos of Detroit, the whole thing was a nightmare of apartheid. But what Frederick Davids, the university's director of safety, found more disturbing was the events that explained it: residents waylaid by young blacks, whites attacked on campus, fights that kept erupting between black and white students. "It's a time bomb," Davids declared. "It's there and we're kidding ourselves if we don't believe it."

At Yale, following the murder of Gary Stein and the series of rapes, nearly all of them by black assailants, the mood was just as ugly. A black junior, David Wright, was stopped and frisked by police as he was jogging for exercise—he'd had the misfortune to run past a dormitory where moments earlier a student had been accosted by a black youth with a weapon. Nor was Wright alone in suffering such indignity. A black member of the singing Whiffenpoofs, visiting friends in a dormitory where there had been a rape, found students loath to open the gate for him. Another said, "Any white in blue jeans can have the run of Yale, but a black freshman becomes an instant rape sus-

pect because he's easily spotted in a snowstorm." Cornell officials described a campus mood in which, as one put it, "the
whites fear blacks jumping on them and the blacks fear white
reprisals."

The mood of black students in the 1970s had shifted from
the militant hostility of earlier years to a frustrated sense of
isolation. Many felt that they were being judged according to a
double standard—snubbed if they tried to join white fraternities, accused of aloofness when they banded together in soli-
darity. Their color could subject them to the most glaring
scrutiny and, at the same time, render them socially invisible.
"Whites will be friendly in class, then I'll meet them on the
campus a day later and they'll cut me dead," complained Lee
Woods, a quiet-spoken black premed at the University of
Pennsylvania. And a black in one of Yale's dormitories declared, "The white dudes on this floor, they've yet to say a
word to me."

Minority students had in particular to combat the impression
that college admissions offices had not rewarded any achievement of theirs as individuals, but merely acceded to the fact
of their minority status. An honors student at Harvard, Luther
Ragin, spat out his dismay: "It cheats us to feel that we're being
judged solely because we're black. It's demeaning to us when
we've worked damn hard for what we've achieved."

Indeed, the achievement of integrating the largely white elite
universities had been in some ways extraordinary. As a result of
the effort to redress once and for all the disproportion in the
number of blacks enrolled, late in the 1960s, their numbers on
white campuses had risen to an unprecedented 700,000. Despite
markedly lower SAT scores than whites, those at the most select
colleges had successfully graduated in impressive numbers.
Three-quarters of them planned to go on to graduate school.

On some campuses, however, the percentage of minority students who were behind in their studies was nearly three times
that for whites, and the attrition rate twice as high. At one
point in the early 1970s, according to a sampling, nearly a third
of the blacks enrolled in Ivy League schools were not graduating. The decimation was particularly severe among black stu-

dents from substandard ghetto high schools, and complicating the situation was the fact that many faculty members were cool toward the idea of remedial aid; adequate counseling and psychiatric services for blacks were also lacking.

The result was that applications by blacks to the elite colleges began to fall off, by an estimated 25 percent or more between 1975 and 1977. At a number of top schools, such as the University of Pennsylvania, blacks in the mid-1970s accounted for less than eight percent of the undergraduate body—as compared to 11.4 percent of the U. S. population—and for less than two percent of the faculty. By the fall of 1977, for example, the number of blacks at Michigan had fallen to only 6.6 percent of the total enrollment.

Even within the older Ivy League schools, which for more than a century had led the way in admitting modest numbers of minority students, many blacks still regarded themselves as an alien presence, token members admitted only to provide white students with a new sociological experience. As they struggled within a white environment to gain acceptance and at the same time to preserve their heritage, black students sometimes exuded a bristling self-protectiveness, leading to a racial atmosphere that was at best a strained and separate peace. According to Carol Black, director of minority recruitment in the admissions office at Penn, "People assumed that racial proximity on campus would breed familiarity. It's just not true. There's nothing with a specific focus for bringing the races together here, and there's a tremendous need for it."

At Princeton, a mere handful of blacks became members of the eating clubs; and in at least one residential college, black students lived by choice in a segregated ground-floor section that came to be known as "Brownsville." Few of them participated in major extracurricular activities or mingled with whites in the dining halls. "When I come and sit down with them, I always feel frozen out," said a young professor and master of one of the college's residential halls.

At Harvard, the eight percent of the student body who were black, comprising about a third of all black applicants in the country with board scores above 700, found relations less strained. But even there, observed a senior admissions officer, blacks far too often received "the coolest, most ambivalent reception." At Halloween in 1977, a band of students wearing hoods and white sheets ran through the dormitories, offending numbers of blacks; many were unamused when the undergraduate humor magazine, the *Lampoon*, appeared with a tongue-in-cheek cover showing a black student shining the shoes of John Harvard. In one instance, a group of blacks refused to live in one of the residential houses because of their feelings toward white classmates. "I think we have reached a stalemate," Archie Epps, the black dean of students at Harvard, said of the situation there.

Since 1968, the number of blacks at Dartmouth had risen from less than thirty out of 4,000 to ten times that number, and many of their demands for more affirmative action had been granted. Yet, as a white senior observed, "You can walk through this school over four years and never know the name of a single black classmate." In 1975 an undergraduate report declared, "Racism pervades every aspect of our college life."

The situation was no more hopeful for blacks at the University of Chicago, where their numbers had been dwindling along with any sign of aggressive recruitment of minority students. And at Berkeley, in a state where blacks account for more than 12 percent of the population, black students in 1978 numbered only about 700 out of the university's 21,000 undergraduates. According to Dr. William Banks, a black professor, "There's a total unwillingness to do anything but pay lip service to the idea of supportive programs for unprepared blacks. Most whites feel the university has done enough and shouldn't do more."

On some campuses, the disenchantment showed itself in an ugly recrudescence of protest.

❲ AT BROWN, it was the student strike in 1975. Although on the surface the protest was an economic one, brought on by projected slashes in the university budget, the cutting edge was racial. Blacks feared—with good reason—that any reduction in faculty and in student services would primarily involve black

teachers, who had the least seniority, and black counseling programs, which were still in the experimental stage. When the
intended cutbacks were announced, blacks marched out of their
classes for the second time in seven years and issued a set of
demands. This time hundreds of white students joined them.
"They saw they'd been treated like niggers, too," explained a
black strike leader.

Too late to save his job, Brown's president, Donald Hornig,
capitulated to most of the strikers' demands, including an annual increase of 25 percent in minority enrollments until the
university's black population had become proportionate to that
of the country. But the victory was an uncertain one at best.
The racial coalition that had organized the strike quietly broke
up. The pervasive social apartheid returned; students remained
conscious, as one chaplain put it, "that at a deep level blacks
and whites here really don't know each other."

❡ AT THE UNIVERSITY OF MICHIGAN, that hotbed of student
radicalism in the 1960s, the atmosphere from the beginning had
been less than inviting for black students. One of them said,
"The whites feel they own everything. They don't like us to sit
together or have a lounge of our own. They don't want us to
have anything."

In the early 1970s, soon after the university pledged itself to
the unambitious goal of a seven percent black enrollment, the
campus was struck by the Black Action Movement (BAM).
Following a week of disrupted classes, rock-throwing rallies and
the trashing of the undergraduate library, the administration
accepted most of BAM's demands, including the goal of a ten
percent black enrollment for 1973–74. Over the succeeding
years, as Detroit's wretched inner-city high schools graduated
fewer qualified young blacks than ever, that goal remained un-
met. At one point, the dropout rate for blacks at Michigan was
twice that for the rest of the students, and from the ten percent who left at the end of their freshman year the figure went
to as high as 30 percent for those leaving after the sophomore
year. For many, consciousness of the antagonism of whites became almost literally a wall. "You're beating your head against

it," said an 18-year-old freshwoman, Marcella Clark, "like you *know* they don't want you to succeed." And the unrest was growing.

(OF ALL THE ELITE UNIVERSITIES, Cornell saw the most divisive racial turmoil. Although by 1965 it had established COSEP, a pioneering minority education program, Cornell had had trouble not only in luring blacks to its rural upstate campus but also in persuading the faculties of its autonomous colleges to accommodate to the newcomers' interests and needs. Early on, the handful of black students who enrolled began agitating for a college of their own. In the spring of 1969 a cross-burning in front of a black women's dorm had led to the seizure of the university's main student center by more than a hundred angry blacks, who barricaded themselves inside the building. When they finally emerged, some of them were sporting bandoliers and brandishing rifles—a scene that produced shock as it was flashed around the world.

Since 1969, racial incidents had continued to plague the Cornell campus. After the Afro-American study center burned to the ground, black students went on another rampage, blockading the campus store and hurling books off the library shelves. In November 1975, after a black woman student reported being raped by three whites, reprisals against white students followed swiftly; a mob of blacks forcibly detained the president in his office for several hours. Five months later, there was a window-smashing protest march after a black college officer had been dismissed. In late 1977, several hundred black students walked out during the inauguration of a new university president, Frank Rhodes. "It'll take just one bad move by the administration to set off the explosion," said an undergraduate.

The lid held, more or less—in April 1978 a biracial crowd of some two hundred students blockaded the university's trustees inside a building to dramatize a demand for more black facilities—but few at Cornell saw an early solution to the troubles. Here, as at other elite universities, a major cause of resentment was the continued reluctance of faculty members to concern themselves with the academic welfare of minority students.

Indeed, the thinly veiled contempt of some teachers for black culture and blacks' abilities only undermined the blacks' confidence: a white instructor at Berkeley declaring, in a letter to the campus newspaper, his low opinion of the work by minority students in his social science class; a professor at Brown archly explaining that the reason so few blacks attended English courses was that the faculty taught Oxford English and blacks only talked "soul."

"You're told for so long that you're not competent," said a black junior at the University of Chicago, "you tend to believe it after a while." Some blacks complained that they could spend four years at an elite school without ever being exposed to the works of a black author.

Such students often met with racial stereotyping or with subtle discrimination on the part of teachers wary of academic plagiarism. A Yale professor confided, "If the guy's name is Gomez and his paper is impeccable, I automatically suspect something. If he's Joe Hotchkiss, I'll let it pass." A Mexican-American student at Stanford, who had received a failing grade from her white instructor, was stunned by the taunting rebuke she found scribbled on the margin of her paper: "Wake up from your siesta." And at the University of Chicago, José Pulido, a 20-year-old Cuban from a middle-class suburb of Miami, cited the case of a professor who regularly mistook him for a ghetto illiterate. "I'd write literate words in my papers and he'd think I was cribbing from *Roget's Thesaurus*. Back would come the comment: 'This sounds stilted, too polished. It's probably not the way you normally talk.' Well, it *was* the way I talk. I went to Jesuit schools and had an excellent education." Finally, Pulido fictionalized a term paper on life in the slums, and the professor, assuming Pulido knew whereof he wrote, gave him an A.

The cultural and social cleavage exacerbated racial misunderstandings and furthered resentment among black students. Some of them found that small things—their taste for late-night dorm parties or for soul music on the campus radio station—could trigger bitter disputes with whites. Others spent much of their time parrying insensitive remarks ("Is your Afro real?") or explaining to classmates that, no, they didn't tan or peel under the sun. After Beverly McCloud, a freshwoman at Brown, accidentally cut herself, her white roommate exclaimed, "My God, your blood is red!"

Biracial friendships flourished on occasion, but too often blacks and whites, assigned to room together, gave up trying to communicate and split up before the end of the year. Many black freshmen discovered that they were expected to cut their ties with whites as the price of acceptance by the black community, and those choosing to room with whites or to join a white fraternity could be shunned as "Oreos"—black on the outside but white on the inside. "The black community here grabs you when you come in and tells you how to act," confirmed a black senior at the University of Michigan.

The urge to avoid racial slights led many blacks to pull inside their own ring of wagons—to an extent that only widened the rift between them and whites. "If you're competing with whites, you know sooner or later they're going to cut your throat," declared another black student at Brown, Ellarree Washington. "We need black companionship, someone to cry with." The presence of black residential houses became an issue on some campuses, as well as the holding of exclusively black social affairs, especially when such affairs were financed by college funds to which *all* students had contributed. At Stanford, blacks caused a bitter stir when they refused to allow white students to perform in a black-sponsored musical play. Just as whites had long dominated certain sports such as crew and tennis, blacks now seemed bent on making basketball their private preserve. On more than one elite campus, some of the uglier racial scenes of the decade involved black student spectators jeering white members of their own basketball team.

Among members of minority groups, Chicano, Hispanic and Native American students faced an even lonelier struggle. "There's no one outside of dishwashers who's Hispanic here," complained a Puerto Rican student at Yale, where in fact Hispanics comprised two percent of the enrollment. Chicano students, mostly from dirt-poor families where English was a foreign tongue, arrived at the elite colleges ill prepared for the competition. "The whites tend to feel we're all dark, dumb and lazy," said one. At Berkeley, the number of Chicanos (17 percent of California's population) had been declining; as of 1975, they totaled less than 450 out of 21,000. At Stanford the situation was no better. In the Ivy League, their leverage was all but nil.

At Dartmouth—a college founded, ironically, as a missionary school for Indian youths—a little band of Native American students, about two percent of the enrollment, in the 1970s proved a remedial nightmare and a source of recurrent controversy. Much of their energy went into forcing the college to expunge all symbols of its early patronizing ways: the Indian figurehead that had once adorned Dartmouth's football helmets and stationery, and the traditional chant of "Waa-hoo-wah," heard at outdoor events. (No one could decide, so the offending story went, whether it was an ancient tribal reference to sodomy or merely an incantation for more snow.) Similarly, the Native American students at Stanford successfully campaigned to do away with "The Indians" as the nickname of the school's athletic teams.

The graduating class at Stanford in 1976 included 45 out of the approximately 90 Chicanos who had entered with it as freshmen. Appalled by this attrition rate, the administration began taking steps to improve the learning climate for Mexican-Americans—a move indicating, as one recent graduate put it, that "at least, they've begun to care."

What depressed a good many minority students was that their white peers seemed increasingly to resent such caring. They complained that blacks were favored in college housing assignments and unfairly benefited from special course-review programs on the eve of taking entrance exams for graduate school. The stir caused by the Bakke case of 1977 suggested the depth of the resentment. After being denied admission to a University of California medical school that had accepted blacks with lower scores, Allen Bakke took his case to the courts—and won. At Berkeley, a campus otherwise known for its liberalism, a majority of the editors of the undergraduate *Daily Californian* supported him. According to Jeff Rabin, a white senior, "Reverse discrimination lurks in the back of the head of everyone who applies for graduate school today."

In the hotly competitive preprofessional courses, Asian-Americans—on some campuses the most studious and the most resented of all minority groups—often performed brilliantly, yet still managed to qualify for special admissions programs that had been set up to aid minority students deemed capable but unlikely to be admitted under the normal competitive process. White students found this infuriating. "They get paranoid about these preferential programs," said Larry Lowe, a Chinese-American student headed for law school. "Then they take it out on us, on an entire race, if *they* don't get admitted." The situation was such that in 1976 the law school at Berkeley decided to cut by half the participation of Chinese-Americans in mi nority admissions programs, and to terminate all participation by Japanese-Americans.

For many, financial aid was the main cause of racial antagonism. Minority students as a rule needed more of it because they came from families whose earnings were low, because it was harder for them to land jobs during the school year, and because they tended to earn less than their white peers when they did find jobs. Allocations at Brown were not untypical: in 1975, nearly 80 percent of all black students there received some sort of financial aid, and about one-third of the school's total scholarship funds went to blacks. Whites who qualified for aid had to take part-time jobs, starting as freshmen, to pay their share of the aid package; but because of difficulties in adjustment during their first year, many black recipients of financial aid were relieved of that requirement—a policy that rankled whites. "We're for equal rights," said a Cornell freshwoman working nights to pay off her financial-aid debt, "but not if it means getting shafted."

By the late 1970s, more and more colleges, seeking a way out of the dilemma, were narrowing their admission of minority students to those from financially secure backgrounds—blacks who tended to be more socially assimilable, less abrasive and sensitive to their color, less in need of costly aid and remedial programs. Increasingly, too, bright underprivileged blacks were entertaining second thoughts about attending an elite college.

Many applied to all-black colleges as less expensive and culturally more congenial. "What's Princeton taught me?" mused a black senior. "If I want to go back and work in the ghettos, how has my education here enabled me to change things?"

For those members of minority groups who did choose to enroll at elite institutions, the strain seemed bound to continue. The policy of giving racial preference seemed to many a potential destroyer of the uneasy peace that had obtained thus far; as Elmer Meyer, the dean of students at Cornell, observed, the resentment of white students was there, just under the surface. The director of safety at Michigan had spoken of a time bomb. He was not alone in what he thought he heard, ominously ticking away.

5

Sexual Anarchy

A sage Harvard professor of the 1950s used to observe that the real purpose of college was to reduce the amount of time spent thinking about the other sex from 80 to 60 percent—a reduction accomplished by drinking cheap whiskey, playing poker, catching forward passes or even reading books. Not owning a car helped. In that day it was still considered a mercy that parietal rules and the distance between places like Harvard and Vassar prevented the distractions of sex from completely undoing the male inmates of the Ivy League colleges and other unliberated schools. By the 1970s, however, with living distances between the sexes shrunk to the width of a fire door, the presence of sexual possibilities had become a daily constant that many students found disorienting.

In the summer of Karen Wiley's second year at the University of Michigan as an honors candidate in fine arts, her life suddenly began unraveling. Her parents had discovered she was sharing the dormitory room of a prelaw student. She'd moved in with him during a spell of loneliness in her freshman year, and what had begun as a snuggling brother-and-sister companionship had developed into a strong emotional and sexual bond. Her offended parents threatened to stop paying Wiley's tuition unless she ended the arrangement. Over the summer, torn between her family and her lover, the girl developed an ulcer. She returned to Michigan that fall seething with bitterness, broke off the affair and moved out of the dormitory. Within months she was off the honors track, sleeping around and dropping acid. At the end of her junior year she left college for good.

Psychologists at Michigan offered the story as testament to the frequently high cost of sexual freedom among students in the 1970s. The "new morality" sowed confusion across many a traditionalist campus, causing hurt and disillusionment.

The integration of women into the older universities brought about some healthy changes in relations between the sexes, dispelling much of the stiffness and hypocrisy. Many undergraduate men were like the engineering major at Yale who discovered that "Gosh, women are people." Co-residency helped to take the fraternity-house snigger out of sex. At the same time, it tended to amplify what a Columbia psychoanalyst, Herbert Hendin, called "the rising pitch of anger" between the sexes. Much of that anger arose from the pressures of having to coexist *without* rules, from students' resentful discovery that sexual freedom had in many ways complicated rather than simplified their lives.

Proximity not only magnified some of the fears that the sexes harbored toward one another, but also reduced the mystery and glamor of sexual contact to dawn collisions in the washroom. Most students either chose monogamy over promiscuity or entered into quasi-filial relationships. For these, the problems became more emotional than sexual. But some men were learning how devastating it could be, in the new mixed quarters, to have one's rejection by a woman almost instantly become public knowledge. Women, for their part, often found the men unfeeling or too absorbed in studies to enter into serious relationships. "Taking on a girl is like taking on a fifth subject," said a Harvard sophomore.

Academic pressures, which had originally forced students to kick the time-wasting habit of arranging dates, intruded even on permanent liaisons. Partners carried their aggressions from the classroom into the bedroom, draining many affairs of tenderness and spontaneity. Psychiatrists treated growing numbers of student couples with sexual hangups: premature ejaculation, failed orgasms, imagined impotence. At Princeton's sex clinic the traffic in disturbed couples tripled over a two-year period.

Live-in coeducation could be a hazardous convenience for some male students. The girl one had bedded on a Saturday night at Yale no longer obediently faded back to Smith or

Wellesley on a Sunday. "If you're attracted to a girl," complained Russell DeSilva, a Princeton sophomore, "you've got to spend damn near a hundred percent of your time with her now because you've no excuse *not* to. It produces tremendous strain." Similarly, many women resented being treated as surrogate mothers or maiden aunts by men skittish about becoming sexually committed. Proximity also intensified the pains of inconstancy. "You're living next door to the boy you slept with the night before, and this weekend he's dating another girl," brooded one student at the University of Chicago. "It's a lot rougher emotionally than waving a placard for some cause." A young woman at Princeton tried to kill herself after discovering that her student lover had spent the night with one of her classmates.

Partners who'd agreed intellectually to keep their relations flexible, each free to date outsiders, became torn "between what's in their heads and what's in their gut," as a Berkeley psychologist put it. The more harmonious an affair, the greater the sense of impending hurt as graduation approached—"like a divorce looming," a Brown University chaplain observed. Graduation week for some couples became the most shattering event in their college lives. And marriage was no longer the happy solution. A Princeton chaplain recalled being asked to conduct wedding services with the understanding that it was only to give the baby a name.

In the aggressively feminist mood, marriage became almost a verboten word. A Yale dean, Rachel Wizner, told of one student who came to her office in tears, blurting out her "deep, dark, dirty secret"—that she wanted to get married and raise a family. The girl had felt unable to confide in any of her friends for fear of being ostracized.

Marriage could be unthinkable for student couples whose strong personal ambitions conflicted; many romances splintered in the senior year over which partner's career deserved priority. Prospective law students, who could once anticipate having their wives work on the side to help with finances, now found fewer women willing to oblige. Women with their own career ambitions were simply refusing to play the supporting role for a partner in graduate school. "Love is no reason to get married any more," sniffed a psychology major at Stanford. "We don't have to lean on a man."

The risks of marrying while sexual roles were in such flux seemed all the greater, too. A University of Chicago couple took their vows late in their senior year. The young wife proceeded to Chicago's medical school, while the husband headed for San Diego to serve a tour in the Navy before enrolling in engineering school. His infrequent leaves didn't mesh with her study-vacation schedule, and she refused to fly west to visit him for fear she'd miss crucial lab work. He ended up filing for divorce on grounds of abandonment.

As women demanded more empathy and gratification in their relations with the opposite sex, male students were burdened with new complexities as they planned their careers. But in most cases it was still the women who suffered the greater trauma in the sexual integration of previously all-male campuses.

She was the only woman out of twelve first-year students in a physics section at Harvard. She dreaded being called on in class, seldom volunteering to take part in working out problems on the blackboard. No one questioned her diffidence or proffered help. One day toward the end of the term her section leader wandered over to the bench where she was struggling to keep two wires joined together, and asked, "Just what are you majoring in anyway?" Chemistry, she said. "To learn how to cook?" he teased. Her cheeks burned as she sat listening to the snickers of her classmates. A moment later, she bolted from the room.

The bias against allowing women to share instruction with men had long been engrained in the educational establishment. In 1783 Yale had turned down a precocious twelve-year-old girl who was fully qualified for the freshman class "except in regard to sex." Nineteenth-century medical wisdom declared that the tensions of college would harm the reproductive abilities of young women. The idea of letting Barnard students sit in classrooms with Columbia men was considered "destructive to the modesty of womanhood." Ezra Cornell, though he founded the first eastern college to admit women along with men, still had his private doubts: at the inauguration of a new women's dormitory, he slipped into the cornerstone a memorandum acknowledging to future historians that the experiment might fail. There had been so little inclination to welcome women as co-equals in academe that in the 1950s women made up more than 95 percent of top-ranking high school graduates who did *not* go on to college. Those out of that relatively small number who went to Radcliffe, for example, could expect to be regarded with bemusement or mild scorn by the neighboring Harvard faculty. A Radcliffe woman who had not gotten engaged before graduation, John Kenneth Galbraith recalled, was considered a failure.

In the late 1960s the move toward coeducation at the hitherto all-male universities gathered force, so that at some, by the late 1970s, as many as 40 percent of the students were women, and more were being enrolled each year. Although the smoothness of the changeover assuaged earlier misgivings,* sexist reverberations were still heard on some campuses.

At Dartmouth, which in late 1971 elected to admit women students for the first time in its two-hundred-year history, the conversion was accomplished only at the cost of substantial ill will on the part of alumni and of damage to the nervous systems of not a few women. One female veteran of the struggle predicted, "The problems will come later when these women realize what Dartmouth has done to them." Although most of the students and faculty enthusiastically endorsed the move, 40 percent of Dartmouth's alumni did not. More than half of these, abetted by a reactionary undergraduate fringe, seemed ready to set Eleazer Wheelock's college to the torch in defiance of the women.

Those who came that first year found themselves up against a hard core of male chauvinists. When they entered the dining halls, they were met by a concerted banging of plates and cups; walking along Fraternity Row on their way to class, they were hailed by obscenities shouted or scrawled on bedsheets hung from the windows. Their dormitory quarters were invaded by groups of male students who dumped garbage and water in the halls. Letters to the college paper proposed that women be made

* According to one account, Henry Kissinger (Harvard '50), then Secretary of State, was observed at a reception in Washington having a whispered exchange with an agitated Chinese diplomat. Asked about it later, Kissinger deadpanned: "My honorable colleague wanted to know if it was really true that women were now admitted to the residential houses at Harvard."

to dine topless at meals, and fraternities announced contests to determine which "co-hog" (i.e., coed) had the biggest mammaries. A list of demands slipped under the doors in a women's dorm called on the residents to muster out naked on the college green each noon for sexual stunts.

In an intra-fraternity contest, a blatantly sexist song, entitled "Send the Bitches Home," was not only applauded but also chosen as the most creative entry by a panel that included the then dean of the college.

In late 1975, after four years of this—"they'd been smiling patiently, or weeping, for too long," a dean recalled—student feminists dramatized their ordeal at Dartmouth by staging a venomous satire in the chapel. The campus was electrified, and remedial action was at last proposed; much of the cruder disparagement ceased; several fraternities even opened their doors to female members. Nevertheless, sexual slurs in graffiti or posters continued to appear on occasion; the number of women admitted to the college inched along. For more than a few, life in Hanover, New Hampshire, still entailed some of the discomfort experienced by a frontier belle when the stagecoach lost a wheel at Dodge City. "It's a common experience here for a girl to be forced beyond the point she'd like to be," said Kelley White, a senior.

After a decade of coeducation at formerly all-male colleges, many women still felt unwanted or exploited by their opposites. "They're not satisfied, and they're frustrated that more hasn't been done," acknowledged a spokesman at Columbia, where Barnard women had integrated virtually all aspects of the male campus despite the two school's separate faculties. A nationwide survey conducted by the American Association of University Women characterized the evolution of women's status on the campuses since 1970 as "change without progress." Men continued to dominate the power centers of university life: student government, boards of trustees and so on. "This accursed race of ours!" stormed a Princeton sophomore, Alexandra Halsey. "Equalizing the ratio may help, but it won't change attitudes." In 1976 more than a third of the women at Princeton, seeking protection in togetherness, had opted to live in single-sex quarters.

That same year, a survey by the American Council on Education indicated that the white male college teachers who dominated most of higher education were generally insensitive to issues affecting women students. At the beginning of 1978, white males made up anywhere from 77 to 88 percent of the faculties at such institutions as Berkeley, Penn, Michigan and Dartmouth; Brown had a score of tenured women professors, Princeton less than a dozen. Women were almost unheard of on law school faculties—they occupied only three out of the sixty-six full-time teaching positions at Harvard—and were just about as invisible at business schools. Women trustees were equally rare (Dartmouth's fourteen-member board had none as of mid-1978); and on most campuses the heads of mixed residences were largely male. "You have to claw your way onto the faculty here," said a woman dean at Yale. The chairman of mathematics at Berkeley bluntly acknowledged that there was prejudice against women in his department.

Although women increasingly made their mark on the college athletic fields, sports facilities for them remained inadequate, and female teams were given indifferent publicity. At Yale, the women's tennis coach quit in disgust and filed a suit charging sex discrimination by the university. With few exceptions, membership for women in established fraternities and eating clubs was steadfastly resisted. "When a frat starts admitting females, it's usually the beginning of the end," explained Robert Wurm, director of fraternity affairs at the University of Pennsylvania. "It signals that the frat is financially weak and needs new members at any cost. The old grads come back, take one look and think you're running a brothel. Wham, there goes the alumni funding and the frat."

In the classroom, women found themselves constantly being called on to give "the romantic view" in discussions of English literature. One woman who decided to switch majors was asked by her faculty adviser whether she was following "some boy" into the new department.

The complaint of Diana Gilligan, a Harvard undergraduate, was a familiar one: "Men dominate class discussion and figure we've no right to ask questions. When I go into a lab, I know I'm going to have to assert myself or get stepped on." Women careerists venturing onto the largely male terrain of the "hard" sciences—math, physics, chemistry—could expect to incur ridicule and resentment. "They don't really take me seriously," said another Ivy Leaguer, Elaine Gilde, of the men in her economics course. Some women with competitive grades were told by their male advisers not to bother with graduate school because they'd probably wind up getting married and the education would have been wasted. And those who made it through graduate school would meet up with recruiters who argued that if an applicant was single, she might get married and move to another city; or if married, that she might get pregnant and leave the job.

Diana Bianchi, a premed at Penn, ran the gauntlet when she began applying to medical schools. "I don't know any good woman doctors," one interviewer told her. Another sat with arms folded and declaimed, "The working woman is the cause of the breakup of our value system." When an admissions officer at a leading medical school asked if Bianchi had a boyfriend and was told no, he insisted on knowing what was wrong with her. At nearly every interview she ran into the same question: How can you handle being a wife, a mother and a doctor at the same time? It was always assumed that she would be the first two.

Minority women found themselves under a double handicap. On some coeducational campuses, black women were singled out for verbal abuse or worse. Strictly bred Chicano women told of their troubles in adapting to the sexually looser ways of the women around them. Within the black community, women were being made to pay all over again for the sins of an era when black males could be lynched for ogling white women, and black females rewarded by white masters for sexual favors: discouraged on the one hand from dating white students, black women would find themselves systematically neglected by black males. "It's caused real strain among our women," observed a black counselor at Stanford.

Even by the late 1970s, some women continued to see themselves as hardly more than squatters on male turf. That the universities now belonged to them as much as to the men could not fully restore their self-esteem nor dispel the feeling that they still had to prove themselves the scholastic equals of men, or better. Anxiety over their prospects was assigned part of the blame for the substantial decline in verbal scores on the Scholastic Aptitude Tests among college-bound women (as compared to a much smaller decline for men).

At the elite schools especially, the "fear of success" syndrome was notable among women. The highly charged competitive atmosphere that aroused assertiveness in males was thought to produce a reverse reaction in females who worried about accommodating their achievements to their traditional sex roles. It was feared that many of them, in dread of becoming coarsened or "de-sexed" by the competitiveness, might finish college more afraid of competing than when they entered as freshwomen. Psychologists noted that great numbers of women seemed troubled by whether they should respond to the blandishments of men who abhorred their politics, or risk becoming superachievers as athletes, hard-bitten editors of college newspapers or captains of debating teams. A Princeton student, Desna Holcolm, concluded, "Women here lead double lives. They know that for a man to be beaten by a woman is the final blow, so in the presence of men they play down their intellect or don't speak up at all."

Other women persuaded themselves to forget about salving the male ego, plunged into the fray and became discernibly tougher, more calculating and less compassionate. The mutation was not unexpected but it worried educators. A dean at an Ivy League school said, "They were going to humanize this place, but as women they've had to double their achievement, so in many ways they've become more like the men."

Sex for many women became the most harrowing test of the new emancipation. Surveys in the 1970s indicated that collegians were "shacking up" in ever larger numbers and that a majority of them were active sexually. A Cornell study reported that nearly one-third of its undergraduates had lived with someone of the opposite sex for at least three months; more than 50 percent of the seniors said they were no longer virgins. "Dear God, it was a nightmare," one mother said of her daughter's experience at a leading college—a nervous breakdown as a consequence of indiscriminate sex and drugs during her freshman year. "She wasn't prepared for this new unruled world." The dissolution of the old structured dating system led to misconstrued signals and differing expectations. "It was impossible to just make friends," explained a pretty Cornell sophomore who'd fled to off-campus quarters after her freshman year in a mixed dorm. "The boys had sex uppermost on their minds. They'd wander into your room and ask to sleep with you. The sex came first before you even made an emotional commitment. I didn't know how to handle it and I've done a lot of agonizing since."

At the University of Michigan, the daughter of a Detroit industrialist showed up in tears at the campus psychological clinic. "She was under tremendous pressure to be deflowered, and by God she was," reported Professor Joseph Adelson, the clinic's director. A young freshwoman at Harvard dropped out after being repeatedly propositioned by a lesbian roommate. Ten years before, observed Adelson, a campus milieu that did not encourage sexuality at so early an age would have protected students from such importunings; in the 1970s they were pressured by their peers to become carnally knowledgeable while they were still wearing braces. Virginity, like marriage, seemed an almost ostracizable offense at times; when a counselor at Michigan tried to organize a sex-instruction course for freshwomen, no one signed up for fear of being stigmatized a virgin.

A class-action suit, the first of its kind, was brought against Yale by five women who charged that the university had tolerated "sexual coercion" by male faculty members. One of the young plaintiffs alleged that her music instructor, after repeatedly forcing himself on her, had finally raped her—an ordeal that caused her, she declared, to abandon her plans for a career as a musician. Another of the plaintiffs, a 19-year-old junior, reported being sexually harassed each time she visited an English professor's office to discuss a term paper. Although the suit was later dismissed, a lawyer for the women estimated that seventy-five such incidents occurred at the university every semester, and a member of the faculty said she didn't know of a single department where at least one teacher hadn't occasionally slept with a student. It was a problem, she added, that could be found at every university. Few disputed her.

A Harvard woman in her sophomore year became so withdrawn, partly for fear of sexual pressure, "that I didn't know anyone in the house outside of my suite." The mere sharing of a book could entail sexual expectations; a freshwoman at a dorm mixer might innocently ask a man to dance and have him misread the gesture as an invitation to bed. "I'll rarely risk visiting a guy I've met in the dining hall," said another Harvard woman. "He'd assume I was trying to pick him up."

Cohabitation, a dirty word in parental circles, became for many students less an adventure in free love than a refuge from the unending sexual pressures of life on campus. Left on their own, students frequently chose to live together in situations where sex was *not* involved. Many bewildered young men and women felt less the craving for sex than the need to be close, seeking security in the rites of intimacy. In a study at Harvard (where in 1721 sexual propriety became the subject of a debate: "Resolved, whether it be Fornication to lie with one's Sweetheart before Marriage"), male students generally rated companionship above sexual conquest in their relations with women. Student couples at Stanford and elsewhere found off-campus cohabitation in groups not only a more natural but also a cheaper way to live. Of those couples at Cornell who reported in 1974 that they had lived together for at least three months, 10 percent said they had done so without engaging in intercourse.

Although the Pill had largely done away with fears about pregnancy, other problems of a quasimarital relationship were frequently overlooked. One Ivy League dean observed, "They play at marriage and they don't have the foggiest notion." The strain of keeping an affair secret drove many couples into an isolation that made them unduly—and sometimes tragically—dependent on one another. The claw-hammer killing of a Yale woman, Bonnie Garland, by an infatuated fellow student in 1977 was the outcome, according to one view, of the intensity such overdependence could generate. The young man who snuffed out Garland's life one night in a moment of irrational despair apparently could not accept the effect of her decision to break up their long romance.

An estimated 80 percent of cohabiting students in the 1970s

tried to conceal the arrangement from their parents, some by maintaining different addresses and phones or by hiding the extra bed in a neighbor's closet. When a Princeton couple in their junior year were discovered to be sharing a room, the parents demanded that they legitimize the arrangement, even though neither student had arrived at anything like emotional maturity. Reluctant about marrying, within a few months they had separated, bewildered and bitter. The boy floundered academically and finally transferred to a home-town community college; the girl dropped out of Princeton, and after a year in psychoanalysis renounced both her parents and the institution of marriage.

Although the fears proved unfounded that mixing men and women students under the same roof would lead to Sodom and Gomorrah, the expectations of some students that the experience would help smooth their initiation into marriage later were equally naïve. "They've been disillusioned. Co-residency hasn't liberalized sexual hangups as people thought it might," said a Harvard chaplain, Peter Gomes. Confusion over the undefined rites of courtship did as much to restrain a normal rapprochement between the sexes as to promote it. Sexual sparring, once conducted at a safe distance from behind defensible borders, was simply advanced to the front trenches in the mixed dormitory. For some women, living on campus with what a University of Chicago professor, Jonathan Smith, called "the terror of freedom," a revival of *in loco parentis* would have been greeted with unvarnished relief.

As the decade nears its end, relations between the sexes on campus have become more relaxed; and the presence of women seems already to have tamed some of the more rampant brutishness on previously all-male campuses. For women at the elite schools the real struggle, as Radcliffe president Matina Horner noted, is how to restore a reasonable balance between their expectations as ambitious, intelligent individuals and their traditional responsibilities as prospective wives and mothers. For both sexes the strain of adjustment will continue; but so will their search for a new social compact to redefine the terms of love, courtship and living together.

6

Careerism, Tarnished Icon

At the age of nine Oren James was struggling through a summer reading list that had been carefully selected by his determined father, a physician. It consisted of four books: A Boy's Life of Dr. Tom Dooley, abridged biographies of Pasteur and Freud, and an eminently forgettable tale of a kindly old veterinarian in Cooperstown, New York. On his twelfth birthday his mother presented the boy with a needlepoint of the Hippocratic oath. The San Francisco grade school he attended placed him in a section known as the "brights," and coded his report card "7–1," signaling his high rank in the seventh grade. He was, in short, being preselected.

In high school the same process continued: A and high B students like James were clearly headed for elite institutions, those with B's and high C's for state university and junior college, and the rest, who were shunted into industrial arts courses, for blue-collar jobs upon graduation. In his sophomore year, at the age of fifteen, James was asked what career he planned to follow. Before the end of his junior year, his father had inquired of more than a dozen universities which courses would most likely ensure James's admission to a topflight medical school. In 1974 the boy graduated with honors from South San Francisco High, and that fall, somewhat reluctantly, he entered the premedical program at Stanford.

After a year and a half of organic chemistry and the manic company of fellow premeds, James switched his major to social psychology. Almost immediately he experienced a vast relief: no longer programmed or pre-anything, he was freer than he'd ever been to savor the rich smorgasbord of study offerings. Though he occasionally felt like a pariah among his more directed classmates, moving with swift assurance along their tracks to professional school, he cherished the next two years, during which he absorbed courses in

Oriental philosophy, nineteenth-century English literature, French Impressionism and the history of jazz. He wrote a paper on Baudelaire, and as part of a class project he went south for a semester to work in the fields with Cesar Chavez's grape-pickers. In June 1976 James graduated cum laude *from Stanford; then, after fourteen dreary months without a job, he signed on as a plumber's apprentice in Sausolito.*

Although far more graduates of elite colleges still ended up in paneled offices than among plumbing pipes, James's saga was not an exceptional one for the 1970s.

Between 1972 and 1985 an estimated fifteen million college graduates in the United States are expected to have entered the work force—and for the first time in history, far too many of them will have been overtrained for the jobs available. Anywhere from a quarter to a half will have been mismatched so far as their educational skills are concerned. In 1977, the Bureau of Labor Statistics projected some 950,000 more graduates than the number of jobs traditionally requiring degrees. The economic opportunities after college had dramatically narrowed; and for the liberal arts majors who made up about 40 percent of graduates, the outlook would remain uncertain if not bleak for years to come. Finding jobs for majors in history and English became harder than finding jobs for clerk–typists capable of only thirty words a minute. "Not much improvement can be expected in the foreseeable future," declared the annual report of the Stanford Career Planning and Placement Center, published in early 1978. For doctoral students, the cream of higher education, there appeared to be nothing but gloom.

About 1.3 million bachelor's, master's and doctoral degrees were being awarded as of June 1977—nearly double the annual level of a decade earlier—yet during the same period the number of professional and managerial jobs in the U. S. had grown by little more than one-third. During the boom of the 1960s, the quantity of master's and doctoral degrees awarded had risen by 180 and 187 percent respectively; and not only were the universities employing more people than the steel or automobile industries, but estimates for the 1970s also showed that one-quarter of all college graduates would be holding jobs previously held by non-college graduates. Bottlenecks had formed at the professional schools, where increases in the number of openings hadn't begun to match the swelling numbers of applicants. Nearly two-thirds of the premedical students who graduated from college in 1974 hadn't been accepted into any U. S. medical school by midsummer of that year. One Columbia graduate, a Phi Beta Kappa, was turned down by thirteen of the fourteen law schools he applied to.

For students at the elite schools, 1975 was probably the worst year to graduate from college since the Depression. One Ivy League faculty member reported students being "so terrified that everything is going to be pulled out from under them, they're not even sure the sun's going to rise the next day."

As college placement offices became scenes of barely controlled hysteria, Stanford announced a series of crash courses with such titles as "How Not to Blow an Interview" and "Survival Tactics in the Job Market." Although during the Vietnam years most Harvard students would sooner have immolated themselves than become establishment bankers, there were now lines of them waiting to sign up for interviews with Morgan Guaranty. On campuses such as Cornell's, the once-maligned recruiters from the Central Intelligence Agency found themselves thronged with inquiries. Though by the late 1970s job prospects had brightened somewhat, the specter of underemployment remained.

Graduates in the humanities from Brown were offered jobs as deckhands or ordinary seamen. Yale graduates in the arts became short-order cooks, parking-lot attendants, cab drivers and nightclub bouncers; students at the university's graduate school of arts and sciences who applied for teaching jobs were lucky to be granted one interview for every hundred résumés they sent out. Other Ivy League graduates scrounged for work as instructors in transcendental meditation or as writers of pornographic books and phony term papers. Some students took on slop jobs for the interim between college and graduate school, but others, unable or unwilling to pursue graduate studies, found themselves mired indefinitely in irrelevant occupations.

Compared to holders of degrees in mathematics or engineering, whose starting salaries averaged $15,000 or more a year, graduates in the humanities struggled along on incomes at the bottom of the breadwinners' list. Throughout the 1970s, the average increase in starting salaries for this group was far below the rise in the Consumer Price Index.

No body of students felt the economic whiplash more than the Ph.D. candidates, many of whom aspired to be the nation's future educators.

At one point, fewer than 20 percent of the 35,000 Ph.D.'s produced each year were finding work closely related to their fields, and it was predicted that the number of unemployed doctoral graduates in the social sciences would total 37 percent by 1985. Their numbers so far exceeded the demand that most Ph.D.'s were forced to hunt downstream for secondary, non-academic jobs. Ten years after he had graduated *summa cum laude* from college, following which he had won a Fulbright scholarship and received a doctorate from Columbia, an applicant to the Woodrow Wilson National Fellowship Foundation in Princeton reported that he was working as a laborer in a pipe and steel supply yard—and glad to be working at all, having long since abandoned any hope for an academic career.

New openings for faculty positions as a result of retirement or death averaged no more than about 14,000 a year—and by 1980 more than 60,000 Ph.D.'s were expected to be competing annually for those positions. The campaign to raise the age for retirement was yet another stumbling block. Between 1980 and 1995, as college enrollments dwindle and few permanent faculty members are being hired, the situation will only worsen. According to one prediction, there might be as few as six hundred new openings a year in academic positions at all levels in the U. S., and only one out of six receiving new doctorates in the humanities from elite graduate schools would get an academic job. Even those few Ph.D.'s who landed positions could not anticipate lifetime tenure or any guarantee of security beyond a one-year contract.

All along, the Catch-22 for Ph.D.'s had been the assumption that in a crowded job market their doctorates would separate them from the herd and make them more employable. Thus their ranks continued to increase as many, apprised of dismal job prospects, found it safer to extend their training for as long as possible. A number of the elite campuses became semi-permanent roosts for "ABD's"—those doctoral candidates who'd finished *all but dissertation*. A Berkeley student who'd started as a freshman in 1963, while John Kennedy was in the White House, finally completed his doctorate in business management in 1976, one war and three presidents later.

The universities, with their vested interest in the training of teachers, not surprisingly were slow to caution students about the surfeit of Ph.D.'s. Senior faculty members, bored with lowly teaching assignments, went on encouraging graduate students with assistantships even though there was little hope of their finding permanent places later. Only toward the end of the decade did the major universities begin drastically trimming graduate enrollments. As a profound sense of rejection swept over those Ph.D.'s who seemed doomed to a permanent sort of academic vagabondage, many sought out psychiatric help, convinced that they had wasted their lives. As Robben Fleming, president of the University of Michigan, put it, society had created "a missing generation that doesn't have a chance in the academic world."

The ripple effect of university graduates wasting in jobs that called for employees of a lower caliber threatened to produce a whole new class of malcontents, along with a highly combustible economic situation. As Ph.D.'s reluctantly accepted jobs that were once taken mainly by four-year college graduates, those holding a B. A. would be forced to take sales and clerical posts that in the past had been filled by high school graduates. These in turn would be forced to poach on the turf of truck drivers and laborers. Members of the lowest stratum of the working class might eventually find themselves bumped off the economic ladder, with possibly searing repercussions. A 1976 report by the Institute of Life Insurance warned of potential alienation among workers, "with increased potential for productivity slowdowns, employee sabotage and job riots." The pressures would not ease, the report concluded, until credentialism in the universities had been de-emphasized and the educational system had been entirely reshaped.

Not surprisingly, many seniors in the 1970s had begun questioning the value of college, as it became less and less clear that to have graduated was to have arrived anywhere. "You come out of here and you're already obsolete," said Richard Greenberg, a Brown University senior who'd enrolled in an engineering course so that he could learn how to repair a radio. "You've no productive ability, no training in how to *do* anything." That kind of skepticism had already taken root at the high school level and had contributed to a disturbing decline in literacy among students entering the college ranks.

At high school, they had grown accustomed to the verbal shortcut of the television screen, and the mathematical one of the pocket calculator. In a major shift, between 1964 and 1974, they'd abandoned such basic college-preparatory courses as English, history, foreign languages and mathematics in favor of topicality and "career relevance." Relatively few of them were exposed to philosophical or ethical questions. By the mid-1970s, the Association of American Colleges was reporting an "appalling decline" among freshmen in reading, writing and mathematical preparation. According to one Ivy League college president, many arriving freshmen were evidently incapable of writing a paper more than three hundred words long; other educators, like Yale's A. Bartlett Giamatti, flatly asserted that their students had lost touch with the language. Yale was forced to reintroduce "bonehead English," the freshman composition course it had dropped in the late 1950s; nearly half of Berkeley's entering class in 1975 failed the verbal placement exams and had to be enrolled in remedial composition courses. The decline in average Scholastic Aptitude Test scores for high school seniors turned out to be the largest in two decades, and even at the top universities the number of applicants with scores above 600—the group from which Harvard and other elite institutions selected most of the entering class—decreased sharply. Indeed, after watching their uneven progress through college, Henry Rosovsky, Harvard's tough-minded dean of faculty, conceded that too many students graduating from that august institution were no longer, by the classic definition, truly educated.

The elite schools, divided between their duty to "truly educate" and the obligation to equip their graduates with something more than Renaissance tastes, waged the struggle over educational values in a decade that saw unemployment among new baccalaureates in the humanities and social sciences reach a rate higher than for ordinary laborers. The crisis had persuaded legions of students to desert the humanities for studies that held out a shinier promise of reaching professional schools or entering such fields as accounting, insurance and computer science. "Being able to discuss Hegel won't feed you," quipped Kevin Marks, a Stanford freshman.

So the proportion of liberal arts degrees awarded in the first half of the decade dropped by 21 percent. By 1976, 58 percent of all undergraduates were majoring in preprofessional studies. They flocked to programs in economics, psychology and biology; courses in statistics and calculus were SRO. At Dartmouth, where English was dubbed the Department of Unemployment, science majors for the first time outnumbered those in the humanities. Of the drop in history enrollments at Stanford, its worried president commented that the trend was leaving students with a lack of perspective just when that was what the country needed most.

At Penn, undergraduate enrollment in the Wharton School of Finance soared; applications to the College of Engineering and Applied Sciences jumped by nearly 50 percent in a single year. By some estimates, close to 60 percent of Penn's freshman class were regularly declaring themselves premeds. Meanwhile, enrollments in philosophy plunged by almost half, in religious thought by one-third and in English by about one-fifth; the quality of applicants for teaching posts in the departments of German and of English history declined markedly. "It's come to the point where the liberal arts student is considered a synonym for bum," wrote Bain Chadsey, a dismayed literature major.

On Brown's campus an eight-story sciences library dominated the skyline while a tacky structure with paint peeling from its walls housed the English department. Throughout much of the decade, Brown's top administrative echelon read like a *Who's Who* of chemistry, physics and economics; its most popular course was Engineering 9, taught by Barrett Hazeltine, an engineer who evangelized technology as the new religion and was revered by undergraduates for his understanding of their problems. Berkeley inaugurated an engineering program for Ph.D.'s interested in industrial careers at about the time its career planners were dissuading undergraduates from majoring in philosophy or anthropology. Between 1971 and 1976 the number of economics majors at Berkeley rose by 70 percent.

Women, long considered staunch patrons of the humanities, gravitated increasingly toward careerist studies; female enrollments in engineering programs at Princeton and Stanford steadily increased. Minority students overwhelmingly favored the "money" courses outside the humanities. At Harvard more than 80 percent of the undergraduates—up twenty points from the previous decade—ranked professional preparation as their first priority.

Even Yale, which prides itself on the liberal arts ideal, was flushed with the careerist fever. In the last days of his presidency, Kingman Brewster had decried the "excessively narrow professional motivation" among undergraduates, two-thirds of whom were opting for business, law or medical school. Yale's departing chaplain, William Sloane Coffin, envisioned the university as a sinking ship, half of its student cargo clinging to a mast labeled "Premed," half holding on to one labeled "Prelaw." At Cornell, a pair of professors caused only the slightest stir when they noted that students could now receive B. A. degrees in the arts and sciences without having been required to read a line of Plato, Shakespeare or the Bible.

Students at the elite colleges were legatees of a debate over the purpose of their education that went back to Cicero, in which the humanists urged the pursuit of knowledge for its own sake, while those who distrusted the abstract argued for the opposite. "To send young men and women into today's world armed only with Aristotle, Freud and Hemingway is like sending a lamb into the lion's den," declared a U. S. commissioner of education, Terrel H. Bell. The aim of a classical education, Cardinal Newman would have countered, was not to satisfy curiosity but to arouse the *right* curiosity; or, as a snappish Oxford don once said, to be able to detect when a man was talking rot.

In the twentieth century, the debate had become one between modernists, who wanted to refocus education on current and future problems, and the traditionalists, who argued that the wisdom needed by future leaders derived ultimately from the great teachings of the past. There was debate over how much autonomy students should be allowed, whether guiding their spiritual and emotional growth was as important as training their reasoning faculties. The modernists emphasized the value of choice, the traditionalists stressed the values of coherence and the need for students to be grounded in a unified culture. At the same time, the whole field of knowledge had diversified so rapidly that educators, and thus their students, had become less and less sure which aspects of the curriculum deserved priority.

During the war in Vietnam, engineering was regarded by many students as equivalent to building tanks and bombers, chemistry to the manufacture of napalm. By the end of the 1960s, many had come to view careers in the fields of government and of science and technology as undesirable. Law and medicine, always prestigious, became even more so: one could serve society with profit. Within a few years, as the recession tightened its grip, bias against business, engineering and science had begun to fade.

The demand was no longer for courses relevant to the social issues of the day, but, as a Harvard student in the class of 1978, Diane Sherlock, put it, for courses that were "relevant to our future lives." Students increasingly appraised college in terms of the monetary return on their investment and expressed impatience that the liberal arts structure didn't seem to offer them a sharper focus on the roles they would play after finishing school. "Not a penny of my tuition went towards my career," Howard Berkowitz, a prebusiness major at Yale, said bitterly.

Alarmed at the drift toward what Walter Jackson Bate of Harvard called "hopelessly unstoppable professionalism," many humanists in the 1970s hunkered down with their comforting credos—*Train the mind rather than fill it*. They bemoaned the vulgarization of the curriculum, cultivating an often rigid arrogance toward the study of science and technology. An engineering major at Cornell, Thomas Wolf, told of struggling with his liberal arts classmates to "secure the right to be spoken to without condescension."

The argument against careerism was addressed in heated terms mostly to other educators and opinion-makers, who were warned that without the humanities society would be deprived of the meaning of its experience. "The implications are staggering," said a Harvard professor. "Who will write the great English history books twenty years from now? The definitive works in the classics?"

Few such educators spoke directly to the students and *their* concerns. Even though in pragmatic terms the history major stood as good a chance to become a board chairman as a graduate engineer, hundreds of undergraduates realized too late, if at all, that they had hustled themselves into academic lives bereft of poetry or adventure, insulated from stimulating classmates and challenging courses outside their own specialties. Robert Ginn, a career counselor at Harvard, remembered his shock at overhearing one night the conversation of three freshmen in a local bar: they were discussing not Marx, not sex, not the upcoming Yale game, but the contents of a bootlegged Harvard Business School report that listed various jobs and the average starting salaries in each for an M.B.A. Priscilla Elfrey, dean of career counseling at Yale, spoke of the growing number of students "with such a hangup about the need to become doctors or whatever that they never really *live* while they're here."

The coercion of so many students into career courses that were often of dubious value inevitably bred hostility. One Princeton sophomore, struggling with a course load that had been urged on her by ambitious parents, landed on probation and was so badgered by her upset father that she became terrified of further study, gave up going to class and stayed in her dormitory watching television. She finally dropped out of university altogether. A Harvard student confessed, after spending her sophomore year scouring for a career track, that "there was no particular profession I knew I wanted to enter, but I knew I had to pick *something*, immediately, or I'd end up a housewife eating Mallomars in front of the TV for the rest of my days."

On the other hand, to protect their grade records, careerist students flooded the playground courses requiring neither term papers nor exams. At Harvard, for example, attendance soared for "Spots and Dots," on twentieth-century pointillist art, and for "Gas Stations," featuring slide-shows on the urbanization of the American landscape; some undergraduates filled their humanities requirements by taking courses in the esthetics of film comedy. Brown students packed a class on electrical circuitry, known as "Shocks for Jocks" because of its appeal to varsity athletes. For sheer mental relief few offerings beat "Introduction to Wines and Spirits," the curricular crown jewel of Cornell's School of Hotel Administration.

A fair number of students discovered after a year or so that they were neither emotionally nor academically suited to the career tracks they had chosen. "I hated it, I cried every night," said one student of her course in economics. On the verge of entering professional school, many became ambivalent. "The exception now is that kid from Indianapolis who's always *wanted* to be a lawyer," remarked James Q. Wilson of Harvard. Careerism not only drove some students to enter professional school for the wrong reasons, but also set them up for wrenching changes in their lives ahead. Because of the speed of technological change, many of the skills they learned in professional schools in the 1970s would be obsolescent by the 1990s; many of the professional fields for which they'd prepared were in danger of becoming overplowed as the aerospace industry had been by the end of the 1960s.

A trendy major called Communications would be turning out as many as 19,000 aspiring print and television journalists every year till the mid-1980s, with perhaps 9,000 openings available. Graduates in psychology were expected to reach glut level before long; and law, the fastest growing profession of all, was expected by 1985 to be offering 100,000 fewer jobs than the 700,000 lawyers trained to fill them.

As Robert Hutchins, the late president of the University of Chicago, once wryly observed, a generation of students might starve to death because they had been mistrained for the purpose they had in view.

Professional schools would probably continue to favor seniors who had excelled primarily in courses other than the humanities; most medical schools would still pay little more than lip service to the notion that applicants ought to be acquainted with Faulkner as well as with the quantum theory. To his advisers at Princeton, Keith Fisher, a 22-year-old senior, reflected the ideal of the bright, well-rounded premed. Because of an interest in music, he had laced his program with courses in that subject while completing the required number in science. Despite an overall B-plus average, Fisher was turned down by every one of the twenty-six medical schools he applied to.

Instead of producing educated men and women, Stanford professor Mark Mancall warned, the universities were encouraging specialists "who to all intents and purposes are illiterate outside their specialized language." Modern educators were charged in a Columbia study with having lost their sense of what kind of ignorance was unacceptable. A new booboisie was forming on campuses, personified by the class of twenty-five students, none of whom had ever heard of the Oedipus complex, let alone Oedipus, and the Ivy League honors candidate who could not identify the source or explain the meaning of the quotation, "My God, My God, why hast Thou forsaken me?"

Beyond the fear and misallocation of serious study that it generated, careerism for large numbers of students became, in Michael Maccoby's phrase, the modern pathology of the heart. In their haste to compete and win, many undergraduates detached themselves from their compassionate instincts. The mania to reach professional school transformed the learning ambiance of the 1970s into one at once ruthless and petty.

7

Grade Frenzy

A Harvard psychologist described it as a neurosis amounting to a phobia. In the dormitories at Princeton, one adviser reported, the conversation on some nights was not a hum but a whine. On many campuses the mood at exam time suggested the Roman coliseum on the eve of gladiatorial combat. Students at Brown besieged the librarian with abusive calls after the library unexpectedly closed over a holiday. At another Ivy League school they hurled chairs in protest during a physics test: several students had arrived late, and when the professor agreed to let them take the test later in the full time allotted, those already in the room became incensed. "The competitiveness makes some of us bastards," said a senior. "People walk out of exams crying, fist fights break out in the hall." Andrew Unger, a premedical student at Columbia, ran into his best friend, who was jubilant over a grade of 84, well above the class mean. Unger mentioned that he'd scored 98 on the same exam—and found himself prostrate, blood trickling down his chin. "He hit me right in the teeth and when I got off the ground he was still snarling." The new war cry for many a student was: "It's not how you play, but whether you win or lose the goddamned game."

For every student in the 1970s who won admission to Cornell Medical School, there had been eighty applicants; to Yale Law School, thirty; to Stanford Business School, fourteen.

In the 1940s a liberal arts graduate from Yale College could walk across the street, file his application with the law school and know that his acceptance was virtually assured. In 1960 any applicant who had either an undergraduate average of B or a score in the 500s on the Law School Admissions Test

(LSAT) was all but guaranteed admission to the law school at Berkeley. But between 1963 and 1978 the number of applicants to the nation's 165 accredited law schools more than doubled. The promise of status and princely starting salaries— $25,000 or more at some top New York firms—lured students and rapidly solidified law as the most popular career after medicine.

Women helped to compound the crush; increasingly they outscored men on the LSAT's and in many schools accounted for anywhere from one-third to half the entering class. Despite the odds against admission, the pressure to enter the best law schools intensified. By 1980 an estimated 200,000 college graduates were expected to be vying for some 48,000 first-year slots, and the squeeze would be worse at the elite universities. The law schools at Harvard, Cornell and Berkeley, for example, were all admitting fewer than one out of every fifteen applicants.

The crunch was only slightly less acute at the graduate schools of business, targets of considerable scorn and skepticism only a few years before. By 1978 about 35,000 M.B.A.'s were being graduated yearly and more than 70,000 were expected to do so throughout the 1980s. Over a three-year stretch in the mid-1970s, applications to the business schools at Cornell and the University of Pennsylvania jumped 45 percent, and doubled at Dartmouth's Amos Tuck School of Business Administration. At Harvard, where graduating M.B.A.'s had been booed at commencement not many years before, the number applying for the 750 places in the entering business school class regularly exceeded 5,000.

When Yale announced the opening of its new School of Organization and Management in 1976, one radical faculty member noted that a few years earlier "the students would have hung Brewster in effigy for that; this time they thought I was crazy for opposing it." Not only had business regained its respectability among students, but a business-school degree was seen as the golden meal ticket of the lean 1970s. More and more frustrated Ph.D.'s sought security in it, and so did more women than ever.

At medical schools the contest for admission amounted to

a stampede. A decade before, some 20,000 premeds had rushed the portals at one or more of about a hundred medical schools across the country. By the mid-1970s, 45,000 of them—a 125 percent increase—were rushing those same portals, which had meanwhile widened only slightly. A third of them, something less than 16,000, got in. The odds on being rejected were such that some schools were said to be selling places to rich alumni eager to secure them for their progeny. Whereas ten years before, the pressure on premeds had been to make it into a front-ranked medical school, the pressure now was to get into *any* school. Numbers of students who had been rejected by U. S. medical schools were now enrolling in schools abroad, all the way from Mexico to Rumania. The University of Guadalajara medical school in Mexico, where some instructors reportedly demanded bribes for honor grades, became a mecca for frustrated young Americans.

Although the stampede had begun to slow by 1978, as students balked at the cost of an elite medical education (more than $12,000 a year at some schools) or became discouraged by the poor chances of being accepted, the pull of the highest-paying profession in the land—young doctors could earn upwards of $30,000 in their first year of specialty practice—continued. Accordingly, the schools continued to escalate the premium on admissions. In 1974, on a spectrum where 4.0 represented the perfect grade point average, a 3.0 GPA or solid B record had still meant admission to a good medical school; not so in 1976, when the median average of the entering class at some medical schools had risen to 3.7 or higher. "Having straight A's doesn't really distinguish you any more," said an official at Penn, where the School of Medicine annually fielded 5,000 requests for its 160 first-year places. Of the fifteen *summa cum laude* graduates who applied to medical school from the class of 1977 at another Ivy League institution, only eight were admitted to the schools at the top of their list of preferences. Across the country, at least three-quarters of the students rejected by leading medical schools were acknowledged to be fully qualified.

Medical schools like Harvard's, where applications had tripled over a dozen years, found themselves having to screen out all but near geniuses. "We no longer run an admissions committee, but a rejection committee," acknowledged the chief admissions officer at the University of Michigan's medical school. "We're not looking so much for the good things any more but for flaws, a chance to reject." Typically, one of those turned down by Michigan was an unusually well-motivated youth who all through college had worked as a part-time volunteer in the emergency room of his local hospital, but had lost out in the end because too many other applicants with his qualifications hadn't had the bad luck to acquire C's in their freshman year. According to Ed Gasteiger, a premed adviser at Cornell, "The medical schools still ignore our reservations about the bloodless whiz kid with the 3.8 average and ignore our praise for the 3.2 applicant who'll make a compassionate doctor."

In a 1975 commencement address, President William McGill of Columbia termed the situation scandalous. The law school on his campus had to turn down 4,700 of the 5,000 students who applied to it each year during the 1970s; the business school, 1,500 out of 1,900. Admissions officers at Columbia's medical school reported that the top five hundred applicants were practically indistinguishable from one another in merit, yet the school was forced to reject 350 of them. McGill went on: "After a long regimen characterized by remarkable academic success and accomplishment, these ill-fated students are discovering themselves to be failures after all. We must correct such distortions or face a revival of social unrest from frustrated students who feel that their society actively opposes them in realizing their destinies."

What the admissions process at its worst did was to sanctify the belief among undergraduates that grades were the end purpose of college.

Many admissions officers at professional schools, ruling out interviews with applicants as too subjective, took the thin-lipped view that grades or board scores were the only criteria of consequence. Brochures from Ivy League law schools tried to cull applicants in advance by advising them that if their scores fell within a certain point spread, their chances of acceptance were virtually nil. Some schools simply eliminated anyone with less than a 3.6 grade point average. "It's reached the point where students have to have a certain score on the entrance exam just to get their applications *opened* at some law schools," said Henry Coleman, dean of students at Columbia. Many undergraduates came to suspect that computers instead of live human beings opened and read their applications.

The era of the gentleman's C had gone to its just reward, but few students were prepared to see the striver's B meet a like fate. "Freshmen today will slit their throats if they get a B-minus, a grade we thought respectable," said a Harvard senior, Daniel Richards. A dean at Yale observed, "You can't afford to get five B's in your tour here if you expect to go on to study law." Too many students interpreted their grades as a statement of their real worth, and staked almost their total identity on the GPA or its equivalent. In some minds the mere fraction of a grade became the nail-in-the-horseshoe that could wreck life's best laid battle plan: for want of a high enough fraction, a student's semester grade point average could suffer, which in turn could impair his year-end GPA, ruining his chance to be accepted by a top law school and, later, by a prestigious firm that would make him a partner within ten years, assuring him a minimum salary of $100,000 a year and lifetime security.

Campus surveys revealed that students in the 1970s spent much of their spare time in the grip of such formulations. Nancy Arnesti, a senior at Cornell, agonized through her final year over the chances of landing a government post in a job area where she knew the salary differentials related directly to her GPA. She costed out that she could earn $2,500 more a year at a civil-service level for which an applicant with a GPA only three-tenths of a point above her own would have been qualified. Professor Sherman Beychok of Columbia defined what grade points could mean to premedical students. "What hangs on their admission to medical school is the probability that each in his lifetime will earn one million dollars or more. The narrow line between a 3.5 and a 3.6 performance can mean the difference between admission and rejection. So if a single grade determines whether you get an A or a B-plus in a course, and one exam can decide that grade—then a million dollars and a student's future hang on the outcome of that exam."

At even the best schools, the system was regularly censured as a disincentive to serious learning and an incitement to students to cut corners for the short-term benefit of achieving high scores. In the ritual term-paper frenzy toward the end of the semester, students more and more frequently larded their papers with borrowed ideas and footnotes. A harried Yale psychology major admitted, "I hand in papers that are badly written and I know they're badly written, but I haven't the time."

The grading process appeared to many students to consist of little more than mindless custom, professorial idiosyncrasies and a simple lack of coordination. One professor's B was another's A. Some elite schools carefully delineated the gradations from a B-minus to a B-plus; others might disregard grade fractions, lumping under one letter the B that was almost an A as well as the B that was more nearly a C. Most students were graded without relation to their peers; but premeds were graded on the curve, above or below a designated median score. On one campus, students would have to give warning well in advance if they wished not to complete a course they were doing poorly in; on another, they could drop the course at the last minute if their grades hadn't improved. At Yale, in the fall term of 1977, 22 percent of all students took at least one "incomplete." The custom at several colleges of not including F's (failures) on transcripts induced students who feared they might receive a C in a course to beg their teachers for an F that wouldn't show up on their records.

The inconsistencies varied from graders at the University of Chicago, known as the toughest in the league, to a science professor at Harvard who acknowledged that he just kept rewriting his tests until the slowest student could pass. When a teacher at Berkeley awarded marks below B to 65 percent of his chemistry class, something like a riot erupted: the students had learned that in the same course at an Ivy League school only *five* percent of the class had gotten grades under a B.

Frank Rhodes, former provost of Michigan and now president of Cornell, admitted: "We use the grade point average in ways that are simply not legitimate to the aspirations of the preprofessional student."

For all the inequities of the system, no other provided a better means of distinguishing between excellence and adequacy, and attempts at reform were largely unsuccessful. Experiments in self-grading flopped: to no one's surprise, the students regularly awarded themselves A's. The pass/fail option, designed to relieve the pressure and encourage students to sample more courses outside their specialties, never really caught on. Students only reluctantly availed themselves of it for fear the professional schools wouldn't recognize a "pass" as quite respectable.

Many teachers, weary of the constant scramble for grades, decided that the easiest way to keep their own equilibrium and avoid unpleasantness was to award generous marks to all but the certifiably moronic. The result was a decade of unprecedented inflation in grading. More and more classes came to resemble the caucus-race in *Alice in Wonderland* where, as the Dodo declared, "Everybody has won and all must have prizes." The inflation, a product of the 1960s when no faculty member would willingly "pour napalm on a boy" by denying him the grades to get into graduate school and avoid being drafted for Vietnam, had reached its peak in 1969–70. The end of the war failed to halt the trend, however. Recession and the threat of unemployment persuaded many teachers that students still needed higher grades than ever before to ensure their admission to professional school and a better than even chance in the job market. Between 1965 and 1975, although there'd been a notable sag in SAT scores, the average grade awarded to undergraduates across the nation had risen from C-plus to B. Membership in Phi Beta Kappa had doubled. In the elite colleges, just about every other student seemed tasseled with honors.

Members of Michigan's freshman class in 1973–74, the weakest in two decades in their SAT performance, somehow earned the highest semester grade point averages ever. The average grade at Stanford was A-minus; at Berkeley the percentage of A's given students had more than doubled between the mid-1960s and mid-1970s. Sixty percent of Dartmouth's graduating class in 1975 took their degrees with honors. That same year, 70 percent of all grades awarded at Princeton were either A's or B's; at Yale, nearly 43 percent of the undergraduates boasted an A as their average grade. By 1978, fully 85 percent of Harvard's seniors were graduating *cum laude*, compared with 39 percent two decades earlier.

What had once been honors was now the median grade for many graduating classes. Cynics described a C as indicating faithful attendance, B attendance with work done, and A attendance with work done on time. At one prominent Ivy League school, a course in natural science offered students a B if they wrote a readable ten-page term paper, an A if the paper was twenty-five pages or longer. In a national survey of college faculties in late 1977* two out of three professors admitted they weren't grading as rigorously as they thought they should, and all but six percent agreed that grade inflation had become a real problem at their institutions; the trend was especially pernicious at elite colleges that prided themselves on their supposedly uncompromising standards.

At financially hard-pressed schools such as Brown, where the number of A's shot up 112 percent in the first half of the 1970s, there was a tacit correlation between inflated grades and the need of some professors to encourage high enrollments in their courses or risk cutbacks in staff, even elimination of an entire program. A lenient grader could draw students to his course like sparrows to a feeder. Some teachers, believing the system to be inherently corrupt, awarded uniformly high grades as a protest against having grades taken so seriously.

Whatever their motives, the grade-inflaters diluted the standards of their institutions, subverted morale and ultimately harmed the very students they sought to help. Bloated grades and expanded expectations, declared A. Bartlett Giamatti, now president of Yale, only served to drive the performance-oriented

* One of a series conducted periodically by the sociologists Seymour Martin Lipset and Everett Carll Ladd, Jr.

student "deeper into despair." The mediocre student with his too easily won degree might find his illusions of excellence shattered on his first law-school exam; the truly superior student could be denied recognition because those in charge were unable to distinguish the ablest when all got A's. A senior department head at Harvard warned, "Employers and graduate schools are becoming discontented with grade transcripts, parents and alumni are suspicious of modern miracles, and students are defensive and anxious."

A number of elite colleges in the late 1970s took steps to curb the trend: Yale resurrected the F, Stanford restored the D, Dartmouth put limits on how many *summas* and *magnas* could be graduated. But the damage was done, and even letters of recommendation from teachers had suffered a debasement of coinage. Never the most reliable indicators of a student's worth, they threatened to become even less so under the Buckley amendment, passed by Congress in 1974, which denied Federal funds to any college refusing parents the right to inspect or challenge their children's study records. "It requires a singularly sanguine view of human nature," said Richard Lyman, president of Stanford, "to believe that very many pen portraits of students will be painted, warts and all, under such circumstances." The potential for a parental lawsuit could deter the boldest teacher from expressing his candid views about a student.

As grade transcripts and recommendations became suspect in the admissions offices of professional schools, standardized tests assumed increasing importance. The LSAT's and Medical College Admissions Tests (MCAT's) were the great "objective" levelers in gauging ability, but undue reliance on them seemed to many students both unfair and destructive. The idea that a single four-hour exam could determine the fate of a young prelaw student appalled critics; it was a prescription for selecting not the best in judgment or common sense but simply the most successful test-taker. Similarly, the MCAT probed certain clinical skills in premeds, but hardly tested their motivation, perseverance, compassion or other attributes vital to the physician–patient relationship. An intensifying of competitive anxieties was virtually assured as more and more students perceived that their futures depended on test performance at a given moment in time.

Students preparing for examinations became so tense that their memory spans were shortened and their ability to absorb data declined. "You throw up just before a test, then spend four days in the bathroom with diarrhea waiting for your score," said a Columbia senior. Others woke up before dawn in cold sweats or were seized with hallucinations. One member of Harvard's class of 1978 tossed on his bed all night before a math final, imagining himself as King Richard in *Ivanhoe*, doomed to a perpetual spear-throwing contest in which he always had to outdistance his opponents or suffer death. On the eve of the crucial admissions test for law school, a young woman at Yale woke up screaming—she had dreamed that she'd dropped her answer sheet during the test and that when she bent down to retrieve it, a proctor, thinking she was looking at someone else's paper, threw her out of the hall for cheating. To ward off nightmares, some students drank themselves into a stupor the night before.

To avoid taking exams for which they were unprepared, students went to such literally sickening lengths as to ingest quantities of orange juice mixed with toothpaste on the morning of a test; they feigned conjunctivitis by pouring salt into their eyes, even cut themselves up with knives. Columbia students swallowed "speed" or diet pills so they'd appear haggard enough to justify being excused from an exam because of exhaustion; a Harvard man was rumored to have received psychiatric dispensation after he drank a gallon of water from the nearby Charles River. There were reports of neurotic premeds who'd fatally overdosed themselves before an exam. At Michigan and Stanford, students were known to ring false alarms or phone in bomb threats in order to evacuate a hall while an exam was in progress. They could then presumably complete the exam on their own time, often in collaboration with other students, or use the opportunity to grill their classmates about the contents of a test before it was rescheduled.

Students might once have approached their reading with confidence, selecting perhaps the most pregnant 250 pages of a 400-page assignment. Now they drove themselves to read every line of every page; in some courses, three-quarters of the class would volunteer to write optional papers in the hope of ensuring a top grade. The crush in the libraries at Berkeley forced officials at one point to give up sending overdue notices.

The heightening competition brought out the worst in students, many of whom spent time in calculating how to package themselves, in acquiring the right vernacular, in blowing up simple ideas or obscuring their thoughts so as to give themselves an aura of subtlety, in second-guessing the answers a professor had in mind. The cleverer among them, knowing that tests were often designed to show up students for what they didn't know rather than to elicit what they understood, might deliberately skip all classes, spend two days of concentrated reading before an exam, and still manage a 3.0 grade average. Or they arranged their schedules in such a way as to keep their grade point averages inviolable with a minimum of effort. In one case that particularly outraged authorities at Harvard, a student sailed through the college on a stream of "gut" courses, obtained a scholarship to study abroad and was later accepted at a first-rank law school.

At the most competitive universities, many students poured excessive energies into developing an intelligence network that rated the quirks and grading propensities of each teacher. Such efforts had long been part of undergraduate life, but seldom had they been so well organized and time-consuming as in the 1970s. "It's all they talk about," said a Dartmouth student who had put his rating research to expedient use: he got himself switched from a morning math section with a tough instructor to an afternoon section led by a creampuff grader, and did it by fabricating the excuse that his mornings were devoted to teaching the guitar to underprivileged children. "I'll do anything to get an easy grader, even if it's dishonest," he explained. "Everyone does." He was president of his sophomore class.

The compulsion to attain the sacred 3.7 or 3.8 grade point average at times made a mockery of the classical idea of competition—from the Latin, "to strive together." There was little evidence of students' constructively sharing their learning. "You can't find someone to lend you his notes if you've missed a lecture," said a Princeton student, James Kelly. According to a Cornell junior, Ira Rosen, "It's brutal and it changes you, always having to beat other people." During examinations, if a student accidentally dropped his pencil, other students would kick it down the aisle so he'd lose precious seconds retrieving it. A Columbia premed finally quit at the end of her third year to escape from classmates so competitive "they'd kill you to get half a grade point."

In the early 1970s a distraught student who thought he'd been unfairly graded actually did shoot and seriously wound a dean at Columbia; and faculty members there and at other campuses were at various times throughout the decade threatened, cajoled, offered bribes and even sex by desperate students. "A few call you up and say, 'I'm going to get you,'" reported a Harvard professor, "and when you read their records you see it's not an idle threat. Their senior tutors say, 'Oh, yes, he's beaten up a teacher before.'" Professors who'd once treated disputes over grades with the curt disdain of major league baseball umpires found themselves having to defend their decisions. Students called them at all hours, begging, badgering, blustering, arguing at length over the interpretation of a test answer or term paper. Some of them became adept at bagging top grades not through academic ability but through theatrics or the wiles of a Philadelphia lawyer.

They insisted on being shown in advance not only sample exams but sample answers. A B-plus awarded instead of an A-minus could provoke demands for regrading, makeup exams or the chance to revise a paper until it merited an A. The more devious tried to persuade their teachers that a low grade would wreck a perfect record in other courses, when in fact no such record existed. Many students continued to appeal low grades for a full year after the course was over. "It's appalling," said a professor at Michigan, "how they persecute you for a lost point."

Most competitive of all were the premedical students. No other professional training was comparable in terms of sheer stress. At the same time, the lengthy preparation to become a doctor provided a sort of psychological Linus blanket, the security of knowing exactly what they would be doing for the next dozen or more years—college, graduate school, internship and residency. To be denied admission to medical school, therefore, was a fate premeds tried to avoid with almost paranoid determination.

"It's each man for himself," said a premed at one Ivy League college. "I know if I get a B on a test, I've killed half the class." Some premeds showed a malevolent skill at producing phony lecture notes to mislead a colleague, or working out purposely wrong solutions for classmates who sought help on sample questions before an exam.

In organic chemistry, the course that tested premeds' ability to live on the edge of destruction, the more aggressive students showed up a half hour before class so as to grab off the front seats, where they could catch every nuance of the professor's delivery and be easily recognized for questions; or they snatched all the best microscopes in the room. Some would deliberately use up the last bit of chemical on an experiment to deprive others of it, or move the slides in a microscope out of the appropriate field to confuse a competitor. The tension was so thick, recounted a Columbia premed, that there was "a subconscious *schadenfreude* when you heard glass break"—the tipoff that someone's lab experiment had been ruined.

Such tactics contributed to the premeds' flawed image on many a campus—"I'd get off the operating table and run if one of them became my surgeon," was a typical remark. Yet premeds were only the extreme symbols, or victims, of the pressure cooker that college had become in the 1970s. More than a few educators confessed dread of the impact two or three decades hence. Young doctors ten years out of college, for example, were found more vulnerable than most graduates to stress-induced bouts with alcohol and drugs. Young lawyers, it was predicted, would increasingly pay a price in heart attacks and high blood pressure by compulsively maintaining the pace set in law school.

A Harvard senior, Fred Hiatt, said of the competitive pressures: "At each stage, rejections, resentments, self-doubt. We undergraduates measure our worth not by who we are but by what we get—what grade, what prizes, what professors' smiles. And in our scrambling, we lose our sense of self."

8

The Cheating Game

Students at Columbia used gum wrappers. Dartmouth men favored the "flying wedge." A group of Harvard students employed their scientific skills to devise a master code so as to obtain the answers to their physics exams in advance. At Princeton one undergraduate stole a set of completed exams with grade sheets from his chemistry professor's office; a Stanford junior led classmates to a cubbyhole in the exam hall where he had stashed copies of purloined answers to an upcoming test in sociology. All across the campuses, the sting was on. Students under pressure burglarized, plagiarized, sabotaged one another's lab experiments, trafficked in phony term papers, colluded on assignments or furtively copied from others on exams. They sneaked homemade "cribs" into class in their shirts and socks, used mirrors, the backs of desks, watchstraps, even their bare arms as cheating implements. Some resorted to "dry-labbing," faking the results of experiments on paper; others slipped through exams, using pocket-size tape recorders with earphones to play back lecture notes or vital formulas. "If I'm in an exam, and I can get a glimpse of the other guy's paper, I'll do it," said a clean-cut-looking University of Michigan senior. "But that's not cheating, really. It's just a natural impulse."

By consensus of students and educators, the impulse had never been so prevalent. Cheating at the military service academies had become a national scandal. Within the elite schools it was, according to one dean, no longer endemic but epidemic. Once the practice largely of the lazy or unprepared student, cheating was now perpetrated by the bright and ambitious in the name of academic survival.

Deans at Yale described the cheating as rampant. "In the old days it was startling to see or hear of any plagiarism cases," said one, Benjamin Ward, "but in the last few years the number I've seen has jumped by at least half." A teacher of prelaw students at another leading Ivy League university observed that cheating was "out front like sex, better organized and more venal." Albert Mrozik, a junior at Columbia, told of looking up in the middle of an exam to see "people cheating openly, talking to each other, switching their answers around, even with proctors in the room." A woman senior at the University of Pennsylvania confided: "It goes on everywhere in all forms—students sitting in exam halls with textbooks open at their feet, coming up and asking if you have a course paper that they can hand in as their own. No one feels any remorse; they talk about how they can get away with it. No one gets caught. Cheating's a way of life here."

In the past, educators had tended to dismiss cheating as a social defect like bad breath, that a little moral Listerine could cleanse. During most of the first half of the century, dishonesty on campus was only a minor irritant because the pace-setting schools determinedly fostered a climate of strict academic integrity. They were more cohesive places then and the student–faculty ratio was close enough that a teacher's moral sense could strongly influence the students in his orbit. Long-established honor systems still functioned effectively, the threat of punishment was a powerful deterrent; punishment itself was almost always summary and irrevocable. Dartmouth students of the early 1900s who gave or received help on an examination were permanently separated from the college. Yale expelled Henry Ford II in his senior year for submitting a ghost-written paper (inside which the ghost had thoughtfully slipped his bill for services); Harvard ejected, but later reinstated, the future Senator Edward Kennedy, who in his freshman year had persuaded a friend to take a Spanish exam for him. There was also less opportunity for cheating: term paper assignments, a target of constant abuse in the 1970s, were fewer and exams were more tightly monitored.

When polls began to probe student values more extensively in the 1950s, however, the growing dimensions of the problem began to emerge: 40 percent of those polled in an eleven-college survey conducted by Cornell admitted to having cheated at one time, and 20 percent had done so more than once. By 1965 William Bowers, in his massive study on student dishonesty for the Bureau of Applied Research at Columbia, concluded that it had been grossly underestimated by educators. Bowers's survey of ninety-nine institutions (including such elite ones as Yale, Columbia, Penn and Stanford) revealed that at least *half* the students sampled had engaged in some form of cheating while on campus—a deviation from ordinary standards of academic honesty that had become "almost the norm."

Well through the 1960s, nevertheless, cheating continued to be rated less serious than such disciplinary violations as using drugs or destroying college property. In the 1970s, although there were no new studies comparable in scope to Bowers's, the climate if anything appeared to have worsened. Polls at Michigan and Dartmouth disclosed that from half to more than 60 percent of the students had violated the honor principle at least once. A 1976 student survey at Stanford found that those who believed cheating was never justified had dropped in fifteen years from three-fourths to roughly half the student body; although students were more aware of cheating around them, they were less willing to report offenders.

The student rebellion of the 1960s had helped set the new moral tone on campuses, the do-your-own-thing syndrome that caused cheating to be more readily tolerated by the succeeding generation; now the trends of the 1970s—political and corporate Watergates, the drive to get into professional school at all costs—tended further to cloud the moral atmosphere.

Cynicism about cheating became commonplace among students because, as a Columbia psychiatrist explained, "for a large part of their lives they've been exposed through television and the press to duplicity by both parents and government." According to Abigail McCarthy in *Commonweal*, students could watch a U. S. Senator, delivering a speech at a national party convention, make up a quotation from the Founding Fathers to suit his text and be rousingly cheered; or they could read about a speaker at the American Bar Association's annual meeting who'd included several paragraphs from another's scholarly paper without attribution. Some students could discover that the reason their parents hadn't applied for scholarship funds to help them make it into an elite college was that the father had been cheating on his taxes and didn't want to risk a routine check by the college financial-aid office. They could even deduce that some of their professors who seemed strangely insensitive to plagiaristic conduct were themselves adept at the practice.

For decades the elite colleges had been less vulnerable to the cheating virus than other institutions, particularly those urban megaversities serving mostly commuter students of vocational bent. Of these latter, according to the Bowers study, a substantially larger percentage were said to cheat regularly as compared to those classmates who majored in the humanities. As the elite schools expanded, however, they gradually acquired many of the conditions associated with high cheating rates at public institutions. The more diverse backgrounds of students now being admitted to elite institutions made it harder than before to get conformity to one standard of behavior. As undergraduates were forced by crowded living conditions to move off campus, many of the personal relationships with peers and teachers that had nurtured academic integrity in the past were severed. The swing among careerist students toward the competitive "hard" science courses increased the potential for flagrant cheating on multiple-choice exams. The rising interest in computer technology courses led to new forms of cheating, causing one authority in the field to warn that society was creating a generation of sophisticated "computer criminals" in in the universities.

Many students persuaded themselves that cheating was their only recourse in a harsh world, the only control they had over teachers who sprang unscheduled tests on them or who rejected their pleas to retake a failed exam. Oblivious to the fact that higher education was never meant to be a democratic process, they increasingly felt, as a leading educator put it, that they had "to beat the system to survive."

This point of view accounted for the often shameless reaction of students caught *in flagrante*. "They never say, 'I'm sorry, I admit it, I know it was wrong,'" a dean at Penn remarked. "They say, 'I didn't do anything that everyone else isn't doing and I don't deserve to be punished.'" A Princeton student, suspended for a year after being convicted a *second* time of plagiarism, blamed the dean for "maliciously" interrupting his educational career. Middle-income students said they were sometimes compelled to lie on their financial-aid applications in order to obtain what they called "equal treatment." Some lied out of sheer defiance. Harvard expelled the son of a former Ivy League college president, not just for being caught in possession of drugs, but because of his adamant denial in the face of incontrovertible evidence. A Yale senior, David Rivkin, concluded, "There's more cheating, but fewer people feel guilty about it."

Nothing fueled the contagion more than academic tension. "If you lift the pressures to a certain level, you break down normal honest relationships," observed Professor John Goheen, the senior ombudsman at Stanford, where in 1976 more than 30 percent of undergraduates and 15 percent of graduate students admitted to having cheated at least once during an exam. Even the brightest students panicked. Disciplinary boards were listening to fewer cases involving students who had cheated for fear of flunking out; of eight cases tried in one recent year at Stanford, all involved superior students who had cheated to protect their high rank. Many, impatient to commit their best energies to the studies that meant most to their professional chances, cheated their way through less important courses.

At Yale, the top student in an organic chemistry class reportedly "dry-labbed" the entire course. In Cambridge, a brilliant Harvard senior, Steven Rosenfeld, was suspended for forgery. The son of a rabbi, Rosenfeld had received straight A's and contributed significantly to a biomedical research project at the university before authorities discovered he'd invented his letters of recommendation for medical school and for membership in Phi Beta Kappa—all because, in his words, the "constant pressure, excessive time spent in the laboratory and a demanding course load caused me to see events in desperate terms." Rosenfeld, as his saddened science professor noted, could have been admitted to any medical school in the country on the strength of his grades alone.

Desperation under pressure became the fate of a growing number of top students at the elite colleges during the 1970s. "Some of them learned to cheat in the better high schools," observed Patricia Geisler, an assistant dean at Columbia, "but a lot of them learned to cheat here."

In the effort to outwit the system by securing copies of exams in advance, students sifted through professors' wastebaskets, broke into locked offices, pried open storage cabinets with crowbars, even tried bribing janitors with marijuana to give them access to examination files. One group, armed with shovels, tailed a garbage truck from campus to city dump and dug up scores of inky exam stencils from amid the refuse. A Yale student walked into the college printing shop as exams were being run off the presses, sat down on an inked galley and departed with a set of test questions on the seat of his pants. Twenty students in a summer-school physics course at Harvard conspired to fabricate their own "answer key" to a set of multiple-choice questions. The course was self-paced so students could retake exams a number of times; by purposely failing a test the first time, then copying and analyzing the correct answers afterwards, members of the group managed to compile master lists coding all the answers to tests in the course. "I'd never heard of an offense so premeditated," said Paul B. Bamberg, the professor involved. "But then the prevailing attitude here is that if there's any way to cheat, students will do so."

At Dartmouth the "flying wedge" was *de rigeur*: during an exam the brightest student positioned himself in a center seat of the first row; two classmates took seats directly behind him with views over his shoulders; behind them, others placed themselves to symmetrical advantage, so that once the exam started the point man's answers could be easily relayed through the wedge. More than a hundred students in a Stanford psychology class systematically cheated throughout one quarter by subverting a process in which they were supposed to answer questions on tests by erasing little black marks on an answer sheet. Underneath the marks were other, tinier marks indicating "right" or "wrong" to give instant feedback to the examiners. The students simply filled in the marks they'd erased, then proceeded to erase and fill in others until they found the right answer.

Some cheaters tried to outdo each other in brazenness. One Ivy Leaguer was caught literally chewing his way to a perfect exam score: when proctors asked why he was champing on such an enormous wad of gum during the test, the student admitted to jotting his lecture notes on the stick wrappers from five packs of Spearmint, each numbered according to lecture topic, then putting the sticks back into the packs and carrying the lot of them to the exam. Professor Joseph Rothschild of Columbia, who had assigned his freshmen a paper comparing the views on free will of St. Augustine and St. Thomas Aquinas, later summoned a student who had submitted an impeccable paper and asked him to read aloud pertinent sections from it and from the *Catholic Encyclopedia*. The student did so without blinking an eye. "Don't you notice anything?" Rothschild asked. "Your paper is identical, word for word, with the *Encyclopedia*." The student, a Catholic, replied, "Of course it is. That's a matter of dogma and we all think alike."

Faculty members began routinely making photocopies of exam papers submitted by students in order to foil a "revision" racket that had students fraudulently rewriting exam papers after they were handed back, and arguing that part of their work had been overlooked or misinterpreted by the teacher. Several schools considered banning take-home and open-book exams because of abuses. For open-book exams, designed to relieve the pressures on students and reduce windy answers, many students were carefully crafting all-purpose answers in advance, then slipping them into their textbooks to be used during the exam. Take-home exams, which allowed students the time to prepare more extensively researched answers, invited blatant collusion. "That's how I've survived," confided a Yale physics major who had collaborated with groups of from six to eight classmates on take-home exams. "It's cheating, you can't deny it, but it's the only way to challenge those trying to screen us out."

Although exams were most often the focus of cheating scandals, the abuses being easier to spot, there was also a vast twilight zone of chicanery outside the examination hall. Infractions included turning in assignments done by others, padding bibliographies on term papers, tricking teachers into accepting papers written for another course, and so on. A Harvard man of some legend made five copies of a friend's treatise on the nature of wars and used it unchanged, with varying grades, in five separate courses. A political science major at Berkeley over the years produced three papers on the Panama Canal controversy, all based on the same research: one for an undergraduate term paper, one for his honors seminar and the last for his master's thesis. He received credits for each paper, as well as the sympathetic understanding of a professor who explained, "He wasn't taking anyone else's work, just maximizing his own time. There's a certain honor in this form of dishonesty."

Plagiarism was not only difficult to detect, but frustratingly hard to prove and prosecute. A teacher with grounds for suspicion might spend a day or more in the library, checking a student's paper against established works on the subject to determine whether the paper had been paraphrased or lifted bodily from other texts. When confronted, the plagiarist could turn obstructive. "He'll argue evidence, demand more proof and keep up his cocky front to the end," said one weary instructor who had encountered the species at both Columbia and the University of Pennsylvania.

Some students became almost slaves to the practice, operating with appalling persistence. A group from the Wharton School of Finance at Penn, facing an onerous term paper in a marketing course, rented a car and drove two hundred miles north to a university in Massachusetts where they'd heard that a finished paper in the same course was available. They located the paper through friends on campus, copied it, drove back to Penn and turned it in as their own. Others recklessly advertised for term papers, tacking notices on dormitory bulletin boards, even occasionally in the department offices of their study major. They plagiarized from previously plagiarized papers, or handed in recycled themes dredged up from old fraternity files. A Cornell junior was found out after he plagiarized his own professor's working paper on the assigned topic.

Term-paper mills were to plagiarism what cocaine labs were to drug-dealing. Out of a warren of seedy second-story enterprises with names like Planned Paperhood or QBS (Quality Bullshit) flowed a Niagara of impressively footnoted essays, ranging in subject from "The Use of Metaphor in Moby Dick" to "The Influence of Developments in Weaponry on Medieval Social Structure."

The papers were churned out for sale at upwards of three dollars a page by batteries of writers, many of them hard-up graduate students. Some companies claimed to have as many as three hundred writers on their payroll and at least 80,000 term papers in their files. "Our most elite writers are from Harvard," boasted a term-paper-mill magnate from Boston in the early 1970s, at a time when a profitable ring operated at that college. Although Harvard and other prominent schools in Massachusetts led the campaign that resulted finally in a ban on the sale of term papers under the state's fraud laws, the practice continued to flourish at universities via a national underground network. Students continued paying premium prices to obtain factory papers for much the same reason that people with homicide in mind hired Mafia hit men: the job could be done professionally at less risk.

"If you're going to cheat, you've got to do it well," explained a baby-faced Columbia student who had twice patronized a term-paper mill in New Jersey at a total cost to him of sixty dollars.

Campus libraries in the 1970s became the target of an unprecedented rash of theft and mutilation by students bent on denying their competitors vital source material.

Russell Bianchi, a Berkeley junior, had his first run-in with the book-defilers after having been assigned thirty pages of reading on Democratic Theory in America for a political science class. The theme was one that would dominate the final exam, which in turn would account for a student's grade that quarter. Bianchi waited a week and a half before he obtained one of the books that were on reserve at the library. Turning to the assigned pages, he discovered that all thirty had been neatly excised with a razor. At Columbia, where sometimes as many as two hundred students would be scrambling for a dozen books, Professor Warner Schilling lost count of the number of volumes stolen from his department's library. "As fast as I'd put them on the shelves they'd disappear. I finally had to yank the whole collection."

The director of the Firestone Library at Princeton estimated that students' quests for assigned articles were frustrated as often as not because what they were looking for had been either ripped off or squirreled away in some hidden nook. A woman biology major at Yale removed every copy of a long reference article from the university's numerous libraries so that she could enjoy exclusive rights to it. "The amount of stashing was so terrible," said an official of Brown's undergraduate library, "we had to go to a closed-stack system to keep control."

The targets of thievery included works on engineering, specialized texts in law and medicine, sex manuals and periodicals of every sort. Among the spoils were books dealing with ethics.

Over a two-year period in the 1970s, librarians at Princeton saw their losses double; in one year alone, more than a hundred journals at two of Princeton's science libraries were found to be mutilated. Penn was losing 8,000 books a year to thieves, and Columbia was spending some $35,000 annually to replace missing volumes, before both finally installed electronic security systems. In 1976 authorities at the University of California at Berkeley estimated that more than 4,500 volumes, worth $100,-000, were disappearing from the undergraduate library each year. During the first half of the decade, the library lost 15 percent of its monograph collection, or about 20,000 volumes valued at more than $300,000. Of its books on photography, a staggering 76 percent had been stolen. Some 2,000 pages were found to have been torn or cut from books each year—"and we know this is just the tip of the iceberg," said a Berkeley librarian, Allan Dyson.

Art professors at Brown demanded that expensively illustrated book collections be removed from display shelves in the library after students had slashed reproductions of paintings from the volumes. Yale librarians were plagued by what appeared to be a tank fetishist, given to excising photographs of German panzer units from books on military history. Officials at the University of Chicago's Regenstein Library, where three hundred books, articles and journals were discovered to have been vandalized in a single month, finally mounted a sickening display of, among other things, a beautifully bound edition of Goethe's *Italian Journey* with its pages and illustrations defaced, a copy of *The Books of the Apocrypha* with sixty-nine pages missing, and a gutted edition of *Ethics and Standards in American Business*.

As universities belatedly installed sophisticated security measures, the thievery began to table off. But some of the more diabolic vandals continued to elude the tiny magnetic "bugs" that had been installed between the pages of library books. They wreaked vengeance on the electronic detectors planted along the spines of selected volumes by ripping out a whole text, leaving only the book's spine and cover. The rape of the libraries enraged those innocent students who were still expected to learn the material that had been assigned. One bitter University of Chicago senior recommended that as an example to others, book abusers be pistolwhipped at high noon in a public place.

In laboratory classes for premeds, honor could be as fragile as a test tube, as short-lived as an unguarded solution. Premeds stole one another's lecture notes, shredded them, burned them, or returned them only after an exam. They stole sodium crystals or experimental fruit flies from one another. "It's sick," said one Columbia premed, who finally resigned from the program. "When two people work on a lab experiment, only one can leave at a time for fear the solution will be swiped." A Berkeley sophomore left a crowded laboratory for a few moments; the experimental solution she had prepared, containing an amount of volatile chlorosulfonic acid, stood unattended on a counter. She was on her way back when she heard the sound of breaking glass. She caught the smirks on one or two faces, but no one volunteered an explanation for the drying pool of vaporous liquid and the shattered test tube, all that was left of the experiment. "They simply blew her up," another premed confided later.

Premed saboteurs would spit into one another's test tubes,

or cough into a culture dish to spread ruinous bacteria, pour coffee into a lab mate's iodine solution, dump table salt or hydrochloric acid into a beaker and occasionally "beaker-tip" down the drain the entire solution a competitor had spent weeks getting properly purified. They knew how to substitute a worthless ringer solution, too, for one they had just destroyed. They would hide buckshot, and sometimes feathers, on lab scales to distort the weight of microscopic items being researched by another, or activate the air conditioner without warning in order to upset sensitive calibrations in a rival's experiment. They deceived classmates by switching the labels on test tubes or shifting the title pins that identified parts of a laboratory animal's anatomy.

The cheating percolated up from the undergraduate level, through the application process for professional school and into the professional schools themselves.

By the mid-1970s, the Educational Testing Service in Princeton had instituted security measures—thumb prints and I.D. photos of students—to halt the rash of impostors taking the Law School Admissions Tests for others. In a number of prestigious law and business schools, admissions officers acknowledged having to contend with an increasing number of falsified transcripts and letters of recommendation. At the beginning of the decade, the Yale Law School might have had a dozen such cases yearly; six years later it was dealing with four times that number. Nor did the academic pressures recede once a student was in professional school. Though some of the heat was off medical students, cases of "dry-labbing" persisted. Business-school deans conceded that cheating was very much a part of their high-pressure environment. The tensions at law school were probably worst of all; one law school publication reported that more than one-third of the students it polled had admitted knowledge of cheating in their midst. Some students in criminal procedure classes prepared drafts of the answers to take-home exams and sold them to classmates.

"Cheating is part of the system here and the system is Law Review," said a Columbia student. "The professor's attitude is,

'You're not worth my time unless you make Law Review.' So people cheat to make it."

It was difficult to measure with any accuracy the growth of cheating—variously estimated at rates between 20 and 30 percent at elite schools during the decade—since apparently only a fraction of the abuses came to light. The rest were overlooked or quietly disposed of between student and teacher; few reached the dean's office.

At the University of Chicago, one dean revealed that for every case judged before the school's disciplinary committee she had heard of at least three other cases in which professors had accused a student of cheating. Cornell's disciplinary committee heard only an estimated one-tenth of the actual number of cases each year, most having been resolved at faculty level—where the offender gladly risked a failing grade from his professor rather than gamble on expulsion by a higher tribunal. "If all the cases I see in my microbiology course alone were reported," said Clifford Cockerham, a student member of the committee, "they'd double our docket."

A survey at Dartmouth in the mid-1970s indicated a total of more than a thousand cheating violations committed by all students over a three-and-a-half-year period—but during that time only thirty-four cases involving the honor code had reached the college disciplinary committee. Of some two hundred Dartmouth teachers questioned, half said they had found one or more probable violations of the code among their students, but less than half of these had ever reported a violation to the dean.

Many teachers faced with prosecuting a cheater through higher channels recoiled at the red tape and the burden of proof required. An unproved charge was worse than no charge, yet few faculty members seemed willing, as Harvard's Professor Bamberg put it, "to take the trouble to play detective," and build their case against a suspect. The diligent investigator might have to peruse every item listed in the bibliography of a student's paper—only to discover in the end, to quote one embittered Columbia professor who attempted it, that "it wasn't the student who was on trial, it was me." Angry parents might side with an accused son, administrators shun the case because of legal implications or adverse publicity; undergraduate members of disciplinary committees shied from making judgments that would stamp them as turncoats among their peers. Many faculty members learned to ignore dishonesty rather than risk obloquy by reporting it.

Some teachers were reluctant to mete out any punishment stiffer than a reprimand or a reduced grade for fear of jeopardizing a student's career; others appeared to condone a degree of cheating among disadvantaged minority students "who don't know any better," as one Dartmouth professor put it. Many simply tolerated the abuse out of indifference. "In some courses a third of the class will cheat, and the professors just don't care," observed Jean Bingham, a senior at Berkeley. More than a few teachers sidestepped having to initiate disciplinary charges because they had reason to believe that only wrist-tapping sanctions—an official warning, or at worst, suspension for a year—would be imposed on the violator. In the same Dartmouth survey, of the thirty-four students whose cases had reached the disciplinary committee, twenty-six were found guilty of cheating, and of these only one was expelled.

"It's a disgusting situation," concluded a Stanford chaplain, Robert Hamerton-Kelly, "and the faculty's to blame for a lot of it. Not many of us have had the balls to challenge the cheaters and throw them out."

At the same time, faculties and administrations found many students disinclined to condemn cheating as inimical to the principles of education or unjustifiable on any grounds. At even the most traditional of the elite schools, where the Puritan ethic had dominated in the past, students increasingly preferred to honor the Sicilian code of *omertà* rather than bring a cheater to book. The bugbear of tattling, plus an inbred suspicion of authority, worked against honor systems; there was a vague feeling among students that personal integrity, like religion or sex, should not be policed. "They look the other way, that's the saddest part of it," said Ralph Manuel, the dean of Dartmouth College.

Dartmouth's honor code, typical of most, reads simply: *Each student accepts the responsibility not only to be honorable in his or her own academic affairs but also to support the principle as it applies to others. A student who becomes aware of a violation of this principle is bound by honor to take some action. . . . If he or she stands by and does nothing, he or she threatens both the spirit and the operation of the principle of academic honor.*

The Dartmouth survey revealed, however, that out of 263 students who said they'd known of one or more cheating incidents, 69 percent took no action of any kind against the offender. The rest had either remonstrated personally with the suspect or passed along a veiled account of the incident. With a single exception, no student had ever reported the name of a cheater to the dean's office. "The honor code is being violated in virtually every area, but no one wants to take responsibility," said a student leader. At one point in the decade, concern over the issue moved the school's president, John Kemeny, to plead in a major address for a rededication to "honesty as a way of life" on the campus.

Other elite institutions, from Barnard to Johns Hopkins, saw honor codes become all but obsolete. Stanford in the mid-1970s had to reappraise its system in the wake of widespread cheating; faculty and students were either largely ignorant of or indifferent to the university's half-century-old honor code. Stanford undergraduates, signing the pledges on their exam books to uphold the honor code, deliberately crossed out the paragraph requiring them to report a cheater. In the words of a senior, Peter Dalglish, "The honor code's dead here, down the drain." At Princeton, whose code dates to the nineteenth century, members of the university honor committee defended the system, but reporting of dishonesties was often spotty at best. ("I make it a point *not* to look and see who's cheating," said one senior. "You know, see no evil, hear no evil, et cetera.") Student hearings on cheating become mired in legalistic disputes over rules of evidence. "The system's become constipated," said Richard Williams, an assistant dean at Princeton. Lorna Straus, dean of students at the University of Chicago, expressed relief that there was no honor code on that campus, "because if there were, it would be falling apart."

In the spring of 1976, the University of California at Berkeley urged a crackdown on cheating, calling it "the most pernicious of abuses . . . a form of academic criminality from which the student who does his work honorably deserves protection." Faculty and students at Dartmouth and Stanford voted to retain their respective honor codes, and to improve them; authorities at the University of Michigan sought to invoke tougher penalties for cheating. The actions, though generally applauded on campuses, provoked sour responses in some student quarters: at one Ivy League school, a student member of the disciplinary committee received obscene messages from members of his fraternity after the committee had recommended that permanent notations be placed on the grade transcripts of convicted cheaters.

An article in Dartmouth's alumni magazine probably spoke for most of those concerned with the issue. "Dartmouth students are both cheating and conniving at cheating by others," it reported, "and for a variety of reasons, many faculty members are choosing not to tell the Dean about the probable violations they detect. . . . If we pretend," the article went on, "to condemn the Watergate coverup while ourselves adopting the mentality that made it possible, we are indulging in hypocrisy and self-delusion. Academic honor is not the students' problem, or the faculty's problem, or the Dean's problem. It is everybody's problem."

9

The Casualties

"Teacups," they were called by insiders—students so brittle emotionally that they soon cracked under the pressure of competition. Notable among them were students who'd graduated near the top of their classes in high school and could not accept the reality of having to compete with others equally brilliant. Cornell's chief psychologist, Dr. William White, Jr., described the group: "They're into a disastrous cycle. They go to class, eat, study, sleep, go to class. Their social skills are abominably poor, they have no meaningful relationships. They've been conditioned at home and at school to believe that brightness is their God. They reach their senior year, they've got the grades, but when it's time for that job or medical school interview they haven't got it, they can't relate. They're so overwhelmed be anxiety they can't articultae or they just shrivel up. We have an alarming number of students in this group, conservatively perhaps ten percent of the student body. I have waiting lines composed of them."

At the beginning of the decade, recalled a Yale dean, seniors on that campus still viewed the world with the springy optimism of a Cole Porter tune; by the mid-1970s the confidence of many was at rock bottom. "To put it bluntly," wrote a Harvard math major with straight A's, "I'm scared to death of failure." Another senior confided, "I fear I know nothing and live in dread that I'll be found out."

The symptoms of anxiety were multiple: stomach cramps, diarrhea, heartburn, hives, overeating, loss of appetite, oversleeping, insomnia. Anorexia became the plague of high-achieving women. In addition to being pitifully thin, they usually appeared agitated or hostile. Many would crumble at an instructor's mildest censure or demand for additional work. One professor was startled to see his ablest and sunniest student burst into tears on being asked to transpose two paragraphs in her senior thesis.

The 1970s seemed in fact to have brought forth a new paradigm, the frightened student. Fear took the guise of work blockages, procrastination, apathy and aimlessness. At Yale, the undergraduate *Daily News* lamented "the lives of quiet desperation" so many students led. Those afflicted might take to watching daytime television or lock themselves in their rooms with a supply of liquor. One sophomore was found drunk in his room by nine every morning. A normally industrious Harvard woman spent much of her senior year baking brownies in the kitchen of her residence hall. Increasing numbers of undergraduates failed to complete research projects and theses on time. "They stopped working and quietly panicked," said one faculty member. Many talented students felt forced by academic pressures to give up pursuits they found satisfying, such as debating or playing the violin. Thomas Pyle, a Princeton senior who stopped seeing his girlfriend out of fear that he wasn't spending enough time on his prelaw studies, described his classmates as "a lot of people going crazy because they can't get control of their lives." Adding to the anxiety was the fear of rejection by medical or law school that hung over career-oriented lowerclassmen. "He snapped completely," said a friend of one normally sociable Berkeley senior who had been thus rebuffed, and who finally checked into the university hospital for psychiatric help. Shortly afterwards he dropped out of Berkeley without graduating.

Campus psychiatric clinics became overrun at times with the fearful and alienated. "I never thought we'd see so many sick kids," said Dr. Ferdinand Jones, a Brown University psychiatrist —"people flipping out everywhere in no particular pattern or theme." In one clinic at an Ivy League school, a 21-year-old junior paced the waiting room, slamming his fist into the wall every few seconds. A premed with superior grades and test scores, he had begun to unravel over a seemingly unmanageable work load. In a nearby office a psychiatrist was on the phone to the student's family doctor in St. Louis. "He's not going to make it," the psychiatrist said in a low voice. "I put him on lithium and got a violent reaction. The boy's disintegrating before my eyes, he's on the verge of a psychotic breakdown." A day later, the student had left for home and the probability of long-term psychotherapeutic care.

At some university clinics the numbers of disturbed students rose by an average of ten percent or more a year during the 1970s. Between 1974 and 1978 Cornell's mental health center recorded a 40 percent increase in new student patients. Columbia's counseling service reported a 50 percent jump in visits over one academic year during the same period. At Harvard in the fall of 1975, the number of students seeking psychiatric help during the first week of classes was the largest ever. At Berkeley, the resident psychologist Richard Beery and his staff of fifteen worked overtime to keep up with a case load that in 1978 still far exceeded their ability to handle it. At some universities, such as Stanford, student trainees in psychiatry handled the less urgent cases. Walk-in psychiatric services and hot lines offering 24-hour emergency aid were jammed. On several of the larger campuses, the psychiatrist had become virtually the only contact some students had with the faculty—for a few, indeed, the one "professor" who knew them well enough to write a letter of recommendation to a graduate school.

In the spring of 1976, a report from the University of Chicago's mental health clinic cited the "striking absence of zest" among students—"that elasticity which we associate with youth." Not only was the number of interviews significantly higher; there was also a 33 percent rise over a period of one year in the number of hospitalizations for students with psychiatric problems, including suicidal depression.

Much of the upsurge in visits to clinics came from Ph.D. candidates. "They don't fall apart in front of me," said an officer at Yale's Graduate School of Arts and Sciences, "but you sense they're cracking up inside." A psychologist at Columbia told of treating first-year law students in "a near panic state." Among medical students, according to a sampling at the University of Pennsylvania, up to 50 percent were said to be in need of psychiatric care. "Students are far more spastic to-day, and the most competitive types we admit just break," concluded Dr. Frederic Hoffman, the admissions director of Co-lumbia's College of Physicians and Surgeons. "A large per-centage of the students in the Ivy League receive some form of psychiatric care and a good many more need it."

The psychically wounded included students frustrated by the depersonalization they saw around them. "The biggest prob-lem," observed the wife of a Princeton housemaster, "is trying to cool the students' feeling of being abused."

Members of racial minorities felt isolated in a world of white privilege. Women raged against condescending male attitudes. There was increasing ill will between the poorer beneficiaries of special aid and those middle-income students who saw them-selves as victims of reverse discrimination. The resentment against bureaucratic red tape, elusive professors and crowded living conditions was universal. Much of the griping was fa-miliar, but more and more, in the 1970s, it was translated into acts of destruction. "It's an impotent gesture to spray paint on buildings and mutilate books, but it's a way of striking out at whatever's nearest," observed Anthony Philip, a Columbia psychologist. "Pranks have always been with us, but there's much more of an angry edge to them now." Ralph Manuel, the dean of Dartmouth, told of students who willfully "cut down whole rows of saplings, break windows and shoot off fire extinguishers, then hide under the cowardly cloak of anonymity."

For the most desperate, *self*-destruction became the ultimate expression of rage.

No one on the Cornell campus saw Alex Rubens "gorge out" on a cold October night in 1977. A third-year premedical student, he'd spent a month brooding alone. He folded his parka and laid it on the ground near the railing. Then he plunged from the narrow sus-pension bridge high above Fall Creek, one of the spectacular gorges that slice through the campus in upstate New York, pouring their mountain waters into Lake Cayuga. No one heard his body strike the boulders more than a hundred feet below, or saw it being *swept from the rocks by the current and sent cascading down the gorge toward the lake, a mile away, where the next day a fisherman spotted it floating face down twenty yards from shore.*

Suicide had been for decades a taboo subject at traditional universities. By the 1960s, however, the number of suicides among young people had risen sharply—an increase of 250 percent in a quarter of a century—and by the mid-1970s it ranked second only to accidents as a cause of death on college campuses. Students did themselves in with everything from pistols to poison. At both Berkeley and Stanford the 300-foot bell towers were enclosed at the top to discourage would-be suicides from jumping.

At nearly every one of the elite colleges, there would be several suicides a year—most commonly in the first weeks of a semester, during exam periods, or during the dark wintry months when a Nordic melancholia set in among some students. Within each of the comparatively tiny medical schools, a suicide every two years was the average. Ominously, there was evidence that the *idea* of suicide had become tenable for an increasing number on the campuses.

In Ithaca, New York, the site of Cornell University, phone calls to the town's Suicide Prevention and Crisis Service increased by a thousand between 1973 and 1974, and more than a quarter came from students. The coroner's reports attested to the morbid attraction of the gorges on the Cornell campus for the suicidally inclined. In 1977, a record number of seven suicides were recorded at the school, most but not all of them "gorge-outs." One sophomore put a plastic bag over his head, rigged a tube from it to a canister filled with nitrous oxide, and in effect laughed himself to death.

For each of the forty or so suicides that occurred yearly at the dozen universities covered by this account, about ten times as many attempts at suicide were thought to have taken place. Half-serious attempts—bids for attention, cries for help—were a regular occurrence. In his diary for one December week, a Harvard senior, Gregory Lawless, told of trying to make up his mind "whether to end it or not . . . I thought a lot about my wrists, what they'd feel like if I cut them. I cleaned off the single razor blade in our communal bathroom, but when I took a few test cuts I began to have second thoughts, then strong doubts, and finally a very basic renewal of my desire to live." Such fantasies preoccupied students in the 1970s, and many discussed them openly. "With more despondency there's been more overt talk of suicide," noted Dr. Marvin Geller, Princeton's director of counseling. In the opening weeks of 1976 at Berkeley, a woman counselor overheard distraught students talking among themselves of jumping, overdosing or blowing themselves away with guns. At Columbia, some undergraduates debated whether to throw themselves under subway trains or die a hero's death helping foil a bank robbery.

Though isolation, academic tensions, sexual inadequacies and family problems were behind much of the self-inflicted violence, some experts suggested a deeper reason: more collegians in the jaded jet age were turning off early from a life that appeared to hold out fewer shining prospects even as it ostensibly prepared them for almost every eventuality except defeat. "They've experienced everything," said an official at Michigan. "There are no mysteries left. They've literally become bored to death." To the Columbia psychiatrist, Herbert Hendrin, the fascination with suicide among students was the foreseeable climax of their having been emotionally dead for a lifetime: for them, only the excitement of daring to die could produce a sense of life.

Yet another casualty of the pressures was the amoral careerist. Self-centeredness controlled his every decision. When he inquired whether he should go out for the student newspaper or the political union, it was a question, observed a Yale dean, that spoke less to the good of his soul or of the community than to his chances of getting into law or business school. For most of the 35,000 young men and women who received M.B.A.'s in 1977, business school had offered simply "the quickest way to make a buck," as one senior explained after filing his application to the Wharton School of Finance at Penn.

The credo of many student careerists, that the university owed *them* something rather than the other way round, followed them into the career itself. They were frequently uncommitted to those to whom they owed their jobs, shamelessly setting their personal interests above the employer's—and seeming at times to disdain organizational loyalty out of a vague contempt for the profession they were entering.

Admittedly, the business world of the 1970s offered comparatively little in the way of role models. Too often, the recognizable figures in the business community were those notorious for wrongdoing. Some students appeared to have no ideals. "And they're right," said Roger Alcaly, a member of Columbia's faculty, "if all that matters is the grade, the credential, to get ahead. Morality is defined by whether you get caught. Many of these students have learned cutthroat techniques that are going to serve them well in business and other careers. Like the Watergate people, they may have learned their lessons too well."

Among prebusiness students interviewed in the mid-1970s, feelings about amorality in corporate life ranged from ambivalence to a cynical acceptance. The attitude was, according to one Stanford senior, "That's the way it's done in the business world, so we'd better be prepared to do the same."

A Yale business major outlined his own exposure to trade ethics: each student in a residential college contributed twenty-five dollars to the social activities committee, and as student chairman of the committee the business major had ended up controlling as much as $10,000 for liquor alone. Local merchants wooed him with free booze and entertainment as an inducement to buy liquor for the college at their stores. "Cigars, wine, the works," he recalled. "There was fierce competition among the liquor salesmen and a lot of money involved. These were real wheeler-dealers. They knew everything about kickbacks, and I got some. Now I know how the system works."

Inscribed on the wall of the entrance hall of the Amos Tuck School of Business Administration at Dartmouth is a message from the founder's son: ". . . Never vary a hair's breadth from the truth nor from the path of strictest honesty and honor, with perfect confidence in the wisdom of doing right as the surest means of success." In a paneled sitting room upstairs Robert Sherwood, a student, earnestly explained how his second-year

class felt about American executives bribing foreign govern-
ments in order to do business, one of the thornier corporate
issues of the decade. "If it's not against the law of that country,"
he said, "you owe it to your company and stockholders to go
ahead."

Other students thought likewise. "To do business abroad,
you have to do it under the table or not at all," averred Louise
Borke of the Wharton School of Finance. "It requires some
shedding of values." A Cornell senior, Rob Hellman, admitted
that if he had made it to the position of vice president of a
company and been asked to propose a bribe, he knew he
wouldn't storm out of the office saying "I quit." He was, he
explained, "too pragmatic for that."

Larger institutional considerations increasingly outweighed
the claims of private morality. At a number of top business
schools, students were asked to decide whether a certain company should fight the Food and Drug Administration rather
than withdraw from the market a profitable drug that had been
shown to have lethal side effects. Privately most of them agreed
that the drug should be withdrawn. But in role-playing as man-
ager of the drug company, they decided overwhelmingly against
withdrawal. It was as though they had been engrafted with a
second, corporate mode of thinking.

Law students, who tended to view themselves as morally a
cut above the mercenary M.B.A.'s, found their ideals frequently
crimped by the competitive atmosphere, their humanity con-
gealed under the lacerating Socratic method. As compared to
a decade before, there were fewer such students thirsting for
the "white knight" jobs in legal aid or the urban ghettos. Nearly
70 percent of Harvard's law graduates in 1977 chose to enter
corporate law, with only one percent joining public interest
firms. "It's hard to detect any overarching sense of purpose
among them," said Professor Vincent Starzinger, an adviser of
prelaw students at Dartmouth. A Harvard faculty member
suggested in less kindly terms that the working motto of the
typical prelaw student was, "I'll keep my ass clean and play
it safe."

Despite the Watergate scandal, which showed up the destructive amorality of a core of White House aides trained in the law, professors of government reported only minimal concern among their students over the issue of morality in public life. "We've become so professional in our area," mused a prelaw professor at Berkeley, "it would be a sign of naïveté to express outrage over Watergate." Graham Allison, now the dean of Harvard's new graduate school of public policy, was one who expressed surprise at finding how many of his law students agreed there were instances when public officials could and should lie.

Not only were students less than outraged by the misdeeds of those in government; a surprising number casually took to emulating them. At the University of Chicago in 1974–75 a number of undergraduate leaders resigned their posts amid charges of malfeasance. The stuffing of ballot boxes marred campus elections at Princeton. In 1975 the University of Michigan *Daily* devoted its entire editorial page to a step-by-step indictment of the student government council for corruption over a period of five years, alleging that more than $60,000 in council funds had been misappropriated, and frauds committed in nearly every election.

In the law schools, the thrust of the instruction was to weld in students an iron sense of logic impervious to emotional claims, and at times the effect was to corrode the moral sense. Law school classes were often forums of licensed aggression. "You're completely disoriented here," said a Columbia law student, Stanley Crock. "Everything you learned about values earlier is stood on its head." Professor John Lee Smith of the Cornell law school warned: "Every moral decision involves ambiguity, but there's a tendency among law students to deduce that moral ambiguity means moral expediency." In place of moral obligations, students increasingly recognized only moral calculations. "Everyone cheats a little," explained a student at one Ivy League law school. "A lot of lawyering is based on cheating. You keep things from your opponent, you lie as much as you can in negotiations, you cover your client's antitrust flank, you cite only the precedents that support your case.

When we get out of here, we're not going to be able to afford the luxury of moral indignation."

Of all the professions, only medicine came close to suggesting an affinity with godliness, yet a sizable portion of premedical students in the 1970s seemed hellbent on refuting the claim. Although more medical students than before were said to be interested in becoming family practitioners in small towns and rural areas where adequate medical facilities were lacking, it was hard to detect any bold new missionary spirit.

Medical schools too often continued to admit those applicants with the scientific acumen that all but ensured their pursuit of lucrative specialties or research at a university hospital. In 1977, 72 percent of the nation's doctors confined themselves to specialties, and 53 percent of those practiced in the more favored parts of the country—at a time when some 5,000 towns in 138 counties had no doctor at all. "The kind of guy who went into real estate because he was bright and wanted to make a killing is now attracted to medicine, a sure moneymaker," declared Dr. Thomas Roos, a professor and premed adviser at Dartmouth. The head of admissions at Columbia's medical school noted a mood of "opportunistic expediency" that did not augur well for the profession. The new student careerist was apt to select as his ideal not Albert Schweitzer ("he gave too much of himself," in the opinion of a Harvard premed) but that nine-to-five specialist earning six figures a year, who might take emergency calls on weekends if he wasn't occupied on the golf links. "Everyone wants to make a fortune," said a premed at one university, "and the guys who say they're in medicine for the love of mankind are full of it. Most want to be dermatologists because they never lose a patient, or obstetricians because more babies are born, or pathologists because everyone has to die."

A young Princetonian told friends he wanted to specialize in treating rich people's diseases: gout, migraine headaches, cosmetic surgery. Another was veering toward radiology "so I don't have to deal with people." More and more, premeds sought the good life as a prime career requisite and tailored their job prospects accordingly. A jockish Harvard senior planned a career in orthopedics because "fixing bones and joints will keep me close to sports"; a ski-loving Columbia student said his blueprint for happiness included a three-day-a-week practice near the ski slopes of New England, with teaching or research the other two days at a Boston hospital. Out of thirty-eight premedical students interviewed at the dozen elite universities covered by this account, only one, a Yale woman who wanted to deliver babies for the poor in West Virginia, underscored *service* as the key to choosing medicine as a career. "The desire to do good for humanity is not a very high motivating factor," acknowledged Robert Berliner, the dean of Yale's medical school—a notable understatement.

Much of the blame was attributed to the selection process in the premedical program. For some students, revulsion against the competitive excesses of their premed years led to a mellowing period at medical school and a determination to seek careers in general practice, but for many others exhaustion depleted their capacity to deal with medicine's humanitarian side. "I felt I had no reserve strength to give my patients, my friends or myself, and no perspective on what I was doing," recalled one Harvard medical student of her training time in a local hospital.

The attitudes of premed students were callused as well by faculties who took delight in debunking any concept of the modern physician as a folksy healer who made house calls—despite the fact that from 60 to 80 percent of the physician's work is devoted to treating minor complaints and psychosomatic fears. "It's an illusion, all this about the compassionate doctor," said the dean of one medical school. "Remember that famous magazine advertisement with the doctor sitting at the bedside of a sick child and the parents wringing their hands in the background? He was sitting beside that child because there was nothing *else* he could do."

"Listen," snapped a Columbia premed, "you can't cry any longer on old Doc Barnes's shoulder. As for Marcus Welby, they wouldn't let that clod into half the hospitals I know."

The more sensitive among premedical students were troubled by the dehumanization in their training. "Time after time at medical school interviews," said David Barrett, a Brown senior, "the admissions officer would test your brilliance, but he seldom probed your character to see whether you'd make a humane doctor." Many students came to share the feeling of Diana Gilligan, a Harvard premed, who concluded, "There are kids going through this place with a 3.8 grade point average, who will graduate from medical school and find themselves in a room with a patient—and they'll still be unprepared for the moment."

Of all the casualties of higher education in the 1970s, the amoral careerist was the most troubling. No one could be sure how to diagnose the sickness of those students who had gradually surrendered their integrity and humanity under fire. The panoply of counseling services seemed to cover almost every kind of troubled student, except those diseased by their own ambition.

IO

Ethics Befogged

The cheating and the psychiatric casualties spurred elite universities to remedial moves which, though limited in scope, signaled an awareness of things spinning out of control.

Counseling services of every variety expanded dramatically over the decade, but so, through the late 1970s, did the demand for still more. Stanford's job placement center was overrun; so was Harvard's Bureau of Study Counsel. Sex clinics were deluged by undergraduates. The University of Michigan offered special counseling to help Ph.D's in the humanities overcome the hostility of corporate employers. Berkeley students, including a tenth of those at the law school, joined a twice-weekly "biogenic" exercise program aimed at reducing stress; another university opened a "test-anxiety" clinic to keep students from panicking on exams. And there were the peer counselors—students who conducted rap sessions and assertiveness workshops, undergraduates at Cornell who inaugurated what they called EARS, for Empathy Assistance & Referral Service.

The efforts to meet the demand for counseling were at least numerically impressive. Yale at one point counted twelve housemasters, twenty-four residential or student deans, fourteen chaplains, twenty-seven psychiatrists, sixty freshman counselors and some five hundred academic advisers—or one counselor for about every eight students. At Harvard in 1977, the freshman class had access to a counseling staff numbering more than two hundred proctors and senior advisers.

To lessen tension, there were courses whose self-paced study programs allowed students to progress at their own speed. Yale reduced the number of course requirements for graduation. Grading systems at some professional schools were deliberately blurred; several law schools stopped ranking their classes and took steps to deflect the competitive focus on Law Review. Medical students at the University of Chicago were assigned to a program within the liberal arts division designed to bring them into closer touch with non-M.D.'s. At Brown, the new medical school virtually assured first-year places for at least half of the premedical students in the senior class; and the class of 1979 voted *not* to establish an honor society, as one way of defusing competition. "We're trying to discourage students from molding their careers on the backs of others," explained Brown's dean of medical affairs, Professor Stanley Aronson. "We're trying to get that aggressiveness channeled into total commitment towards the patient."

There were other, smaller efforts to restore some humaneness to college life. A Princeton housemaster every month gave a dinner party in his quarters for all students born during that month; the college chapel opened its doors from 11 P.M. to midnight for a concert of organ music. Dartmouth started mini-Outward Bound programs to bring freshmen together. Cornell hired a therapist to work one-on-one with emotionally troubled students, and furnished "relaxation" tape recordings to help them unwind. At the University of Pennsylvania, a master chess player was invited to take up residence in one of the dormitories, where in nightly games he took on up to twenty students at a time.

However well intentioned, all this seldom amounted to more than cosmetic improvement. "The biggest sign of weakness is in relation to advising," Stanford's president, Richard Lyman, remarked in early 1978. "A clear majority of the students don't feel they get a very good deal." Counselors often seemed more clinical than caring, or too handy with bland nostrums instead of hard advice. The process didn't so much exorcise the tensions as make students feel temporarily more comfortable; accommodation, not challenge, was frequently the rule. A sophomore with doubts about himself might be advised to consider homosexuality as a preference rather than as a problem to be surmounted. "The universities are over-counseled, extraordinarily so," declared the University of Michigan psychologist Joseph Adelson, "and the undergraduates, abandoned by faculty and administration, are being bought off by these services."

What no one seemed able to provide was a searching dialogue with students concerning larger values beyond academic glory and a career, despite indications that a sizable majority of students would have welcomed some attention to their emotional growth.* "No one ever suggests, 'Stop. Reconsider. What *are* your goals and what *is* it you're trying to achieve here?' " was the complaint of Jeffrey Leonard, an editor of the Harvard *Crimson*. A Yale senior, David Zweig, declared: "Few of us even stop to think about the lack of moral values here. You live a preprofessional existence that provides its own moral answers—700 scores on the law school admissions tests and a 3.5 grade point average. Those are our values."

The distinction between good and evil was no longer simply "perceived by the heart," in Solzhenitsyn's phrase. The buck had been passed, all the way from childhood to college age. It was an article of faith, however misplaced, that students' values had been firmly established by the time they entered graduate school. At each level, from professional school down through kindergarten to the parents themselves, it was assumed that character and discipline had already been instilled.

Meanwhile, all through the 1970s more and more students had become in effect parentless—traumatized by divorce, ignored by professional parents, or brought up by mothers and fathers who were at best dubious models. Before tax checks were instituted, nearly a fifth of the parents applying for aid at the University of Chicago were misrepresenting their income by $1,000 or more, and the phenomenon appeared to be nationwide. "An earlier generation might have assumed that the basic tenets of morality would have been learned by students at their parents' knee," observed Chicago's dean of college, Charles Oxnard, "or it would have been beaten into them. No longer."

The primary and secondary schools appeared similarly to have relinquished their moral hold on the young. "The administra-

* According to a 1973 Carnegie Commission survey, 83 percent of college students in the U. S. favored such a trend.

tion assumes that students coming here have a code of values about cheating, but they don't," said Fred Wall, the president of Dartmouth's 1976 senior class. In many of the lower schools, the rate of cheating ranged as high as a sickening 88 percent.

In earlier times, when the colleges' function of *in loco parentis* remained unquestioned, developing conscience in students had been a centerpiece of university life. College presidents regularly preached the accepted principles of the age; students attended compulsory chapel; the atmosphere was still redolent of Puritanism in the many leading colleges which had been founded to train students for the ministry or teaching. As vast social changes occurred and the colleges increasingly admitted students from diverse backgrounds, headed for a wider range of careers, many traditional values became more susceptible to question. At the same time, probing classroom discussions were replaced by impersonal survey courses, which might acquaint a student with the long tradition of ethical philosophy but often did little to stimulate close reasoning on the subject. Such courses seemed more and more irrelevant to the complex moral dilemmas that students had to confront in their own lives.

In the no-fault, guilt-free new social order, the university's moral authority had languished. "Character is a word that's dropped out of the university's vocabulary," said Norman Jacobson, a political science professor at Berkeley. College disciplinary committees fussed interminably over what once would have been seen as clear-cut instances of academic dishonesty. In the case of a Princeton student who persisted in copying transcripts of faculty lectures and selling them to classmates, no one individual, it seemed, wanted to take the responsibility for disciplining the offender. "It's madness," declared Ernest Gordon, the university's senior theologian. "Not long ago, a dean would simply have said, 'Stop it or get out.' "

To a man, chaplains at the leading colleges blamed their schools for failing to rekindle a sense of moral purpose among students—for "benign neglect," as Yale's Lutheran chaplain, Thomas Chittick, called it. "The wraps are off, there's no party line on morals," acknowledged Dartmouth's chaplain, Warner Traynham. The Episcopal chaplain at Princeton depicted that campus as a place where "people bend so far backwards to be nonabsolutist, they avoid all moral commitment." Harvard, according to its principal religious adviser, Peter Gomes, was so wary of sounding didactic that it hadn't taken a really fervent moral position on anything "since it condemned the Salem witchcraft trials." In early 1978 a deeply concerned Harvard president, Derek Bok, admitted, "We have little reason to believe that Harvard does much to promote moral reasoning, let alone moral conduct."

Not only was moral neutrality espoused; it was also considered preferable to hide your feelings about a roommate's smoking or sexual behavior than to be thought a moralizer. In a Harvard course on the rise of Nazism, students' disinclination to assign blame for the atrocities made one observer ask whether, had they been sitting in judgment at Nuremberg, they wouldn't have acquitted all the defendants. "If you wrote a book attacking Ghengis Khan, students would question if there wasn't a good side to him," said an angry Princeton professor.

Increasingly, too, students tended to absolve themselves of personal responsibility for dishonesty, blaming it on financial hardship, academic pressures or ethnic disadvantage. Those thousands who welshed on their college loans were less culpable, maintained one senior, than the society that had forced them into such an untenable situation. Cheating could somehow be rationalized away, leaving the individual blameless. Robben Fleming, president of the University of Michigan, expressed shock at the number of young Watergate felons who had been graduated from distinguished universities. "Why did we have so little impact on them?" he wondered.

By the middle of the decade an overwhelming majority of Americans favored instruction on moral issues in their schools,* but within the leading universities the momentum was slow in building.

Some educators begged off with the excuse that the universities only reflected society's general corrosion and should not be held accountable for it. Many balked on the grounds that values were impossible to teach, that secular faculties were

---

* According to a Gallup poll taken in April 1976, 79 percent of those interviewed supported the idea.

ill equipped to do so, and that in any event the need remained unproved. Students could probably get more out of watching a television documentary on white-collar crime than from anything the faculty could tell them, argued the vice dean of Pennsylvania's Wharton School of Finance. The jails were full of people who had passed ethics courses, the dean of Stanford's business school added. If a student hadn't character or moral perspective, the college couldn't provide them; nor, with its limited funds and time, should it attempt to do so. Morality was simply unsusceptible to objective analysis like mathematics, insisted a University of Chicago professor. "You can't teach it the way you teach the clarinet. We lack the language to discuss right and wrong."

Those who favored a moral reformation in the classroom challenged the universities to be more than servants of the status quo. They attacked the assumption that students, as one Dartmouth alumnus argued, were "no worse than the leaders they're being trained to succeed," that "in the classroom, as in the Oval Office, cheating is an inescapable fact of life." Faculties had to start moving ethics instruction out of the musty religion and philosophy departments and design imaginative problem-oriented courses that emphasized everyday moral choices, that encouraged the discussion of moral ambiguities. Too often, as Sissela Bok, a teacher of ethics, pointed out in her book on lying, college ethics courses had left students "confirmed in their suspicion that moral choice is murky and best left to intuition." Above all, it was argued, more teachers had to involve themselves personally, recognizing, as one of them put it, that it would be more honest to admit the near impossibility of separating their values from what and how they taught. A prominent Harvard educator concluded, "Until teachers are willing to step out from behind their shield of academic objectivity, showing students by example what they believe is right and wrong, nothing will happen."

Even by the late 1970s, although ethics courses had begun appearing throughout colleges and professional schools, the fundamental skepticism of teachers about injecting values into their classes remained. Many shied from involvement for fear of sounding like scolds and inviting their students' ridicule.

"You used to have teachers here who were consciences," a Yale senior said, "but no more unless they want to risk heckling." And Donald Stokes, the dean of Princeton's Woodrow Wilson School of Public and International Affairs, declared, "At institutions like this there's a natural suspicion of teaching Sunday school." The continued detachment among teachers was disturbing to those students who sought in their classrooms not moral neuters but models of committed integrity, men and women willing to assume a moral stance.

At Brown, students in a government course taught by a former CIA executive could absorb all the intricacies of espionage—from the obligatory vial of curare to sabotage of enemy satellites—and never be asked to consider the morality of it all. Business students at Harvard and Yale could listen to instructors explain the methods of double-entry bookkeeping without offering any serious assessment of the practice. A Princeton senior, Charles Ballard, described how one of his professors went about preparing the next generation of tax accountants: "He showed us all the creative ways to find loopholes, telling us how to fight stockholders who want dividends and the government who wants tax monies. He told us in effect that the government rips off taxpayers, so we accountants would be free to play the game of loopholes with them."

Rarely had the need for ethics training been as urgent as it now was in the professional schools. A Gallup poll taken in September 1977 showed that less than 20 percent of Americans had confidence in the honesty of government servants and business executives, one-quarter in the honesty of lawyers, and only half in that of doctors. Garbage collectors rated more confidence than political leaders. Between 1970 and 1976, indictments of public officials by Federal grand juries had risen 500 percent. The roster of those indicted, convicted or otherwise disgraced included a President, a Vice President, three Cabinet members (one of them the highest legal officer in the land), three governors, thirty-four state legislators, twenty judges, five state attorneys general, twenty-eight mayors and eleven district attorneys.

Out of the Watergate era had emerged a hero or two, such

as Archibald Cox of Harvard. But what of Richard Kleindienst, the Harvard-educated attorney general who lied under oath at his confirmation hearing; or Charles Colson (Brown '53), Nixon's convicted political hit man; or former CIA chief Richard Helms (Williams '35), along with other public servants, many of them trained at elite colleges, who deceived Congress in the name of national security or who initiated illegal wiretaps on citizens? Few acted out of wholly venal motives; most simply exercised wrong moral choices at the crucial moment. Some younger ones, like the hapless Jeb Magruder (Williams '58), appeared to have wandered into the jackals' den with no ethical compass at all. "I lived fifty years of my life without ever really coming to grips with the very basic question of what is and is not right and wrong," acknowledged John Ehrlichman, who had once argued issues as a member of the Stanford Law School debating team.

Few of the well-spoken young witnesses who testified before Senator Sam Ervin's select committee indicated any understanding or appreciation of democratic principles. In the words of a special panel commissioned to report on the implications of the Senate Watergate hearings, "They had not learned in secondary school or in college or in law school that there is something special about public office and public responsibility."*

Most of the country's leading colleges and professional schools now offered courses in ethics, some of the traditional sort and others emphasizing practical applications. But even where it had been incorporated into the curriculum, few business or medical schools made the course mandatory. Among law schools the exception was a place such as Cornell, which following the Watergate episode established a special Center for Law, Ethics and Religion. "Some days I feel confident, some days terribly unconfident," said Professor John Lee Smith, the director of the ethics program there. "We're trying to create an eddy and we're swimming upstream."

After eighteen lawyers connected with the Watergate affair

* *Watergate: The Implications for Responsible Government.* Report by a Panel of the National Academy of Public Administration, for the Senate Select Committee on Presidential Campaign Activities, March 1974.

had been disbarred or disciplined, the American Bar Association, a group not generally known for its progressivism, had in fact called on law schools to inaugurate special courses in legal ethics. When Harvard Law School, the nation's most prestigious, ordained in 1975 that its students would henceforth be required to take a course in Professional Responsibility, it was the first time in a quarter century that a new requirement had been added to the school's curriculum; in a sense, it symbolized the legal fraternity's glacial progress in coming to terms with the concept of public accountability. The canons embodied in the existing code of ethics were seen by many as primarily serving the rights of lawyers, shielding them from public criticism and fattening their fees. Within the law schools, generations of students were trained for an adversary system in which the rules tended to be unrelated to ordinary notions of morality, with little stress on the lawyers' transcendent obligations to their own and the public conscience.

The same was true of leading schools of business. Less than three-fourths of American businessmen, according to one survey, considered honesty important to their work. In the drive to amass profits, as with aiming for good grades, the temptation was great to legitimize all kinds of dubious practices, from doctored accounting to laundered funds. By one estimate, the amount of money secretly pocketed through corporate bribery and kickbacks ran as high as $15 billion a year in the 1970s, or about one percent of the Gross National Product. Company presidents who'd disgraced themselves in the eyes of the public might be hailed as martyrs by their colleagues, given wrist-slap fines—and not infrequently they kept their jobs. Nearly half the business leaders who were polled following the Lockheed–Gulf Oil bribery scandal of 1975 said they thought companies should continue to pay bribes to foreign officials if such bribes had been the custom. The mandarins of business and finance couldn't even agree on whether a professional code of ethics was necessary, as it is for lawyers and doctors, much less what such a code should include.*

---

* After the Bert Lance affair of 1977—in which the President's most trusted economic adviser was revealed to have engaged in massive over-

With so much confusion on the outside, the task of providing future business executives with moral antennae seemed quixotic. "This school pays lip service to ethics, but that's about all," declared David McNiff, a graduate student at the Wharton School of Finance.

When Milton Friedman, the noted University of Chicago economist, defended one dubious practice as a necessary evil of doing business, the dean of Stanford's business school, Arjay Miller, inquired, "Would you pay $10,000 in bribes to ensure your tenure?" Yet few teachers of business seemed willing to expose their own feelings on questions of ethics. "I never put my values into that classroom," said Wayne Broehl, who taught a course in corporate ethics at Dartmouth's Tuck School of Business Administration. In later years, Broehl agreed, most of his students would confront moral issues by carefully weighing their options rather than acting from an instinctive sense of right. "We teach there are no right or wrong answers," said a young Harvard Business School officer. "You act on what you can live with." It was always a question of deciding what makes sense, explained Donald Carroll, the dean of Wharton—not what *feels* right. Some teachers were clearly out of their element in any kind of ethical dialogue. Musing on the reports of corporate bribery, an economics professor at Princeton said he wasn't sure he wouldn't have done "the same things those businessmen did. You're under a hell of a lot of pressure from stockholders."

The authors of a 1976 survey of more than a hundred management students on their attitudes toward corporate bribery wrote: "We were disheartened to find so many who were willing to justify such a practice on the grounds of 'Everybody does it.' Such responses raise the question of what we as educators can do, if anything, to instill a greater sense of morality into the day-to-day practice of business. . . . There may indeed be little we can do."

Medical schools appeared equally slow to recognize the need

---

drafts and other questionable practices while head of a Georgia bank—officials at one of New York's biggest banks gave up an attempt to explain to their employees exactly what Lance had done and why it was wrong: they couldn't decide whether Lance had acted illegally, unethically, improperly or just outrageously.

for change, despite contentions that too many physicians showed more technique than heart, despite a 1,000-percent jump in doctors' fees within a generation, and despite charges of fee-splitting, of padded Medicaid claims, and of having performed two million allegedly unnecessary operations each year —leading, by one estimate, to 15,000 preventable deaths.

The number of medical malpractice suits had gone from 26,500 in 1970 to some 46,000 by the middle of the decade. Many of these were thought to stem from a basic distrust of doctors as caring individuals. In 1977, professional nurses across the country were asked to rate doctors on the quality of psychological support they gave to their patients in hospital: 77 percent of the nurses rated the doctors' performance to be no better than fair.

Although by the late 1970s nearly every medical school was offering at least one ethics course, the machinery was still geared to producing superlative technicians, despite the fact that almost daily, in making decisions about their patients, the *moral* judgments facing doctors were likely to be far more difficult than the scientific or medical ones. There seemed to be little room in the curriculum for serious consideration of the doctor–patient relationship or such questions raised by the biomedical revolution as that of permitting unlimited genetics research, or the right to die, or the rights of pregnant women and of patients in general. Relatively little effort was made to sensitize students to the more troubling human questions of medical practice. Should doctors lie or dissemble to patients for their "own good"? (The requirement to be honest with patients has no place in medical oaths and is often ignored in medical teaching.) Should they report colleagues who had committed medically incompetent acts? (Yes, according to the professional code, though in fact few doctors do.)

The clinical training in a medical student's later years might expose him to such issues, but it could also impress on him the callousness within the profession. A young graduate of the Harvard Medical School, Carmen Puliafito, recalled witnessing as a student the last hours in a Boston hospital of a terminally ill patient who'd requested euthanasia. The doctors had delayed withdrawing the patient's life-support system until they

learned whether the patient's family would donate his kidneys
to the hospital after death. "It was cold-blooded," Puliafito
said, "keeping this guy plugged in, waiting to hear if we could
harvest his kidneys." Ethics, he added, was something you
caught on the fly at medical school, if you were even aware of
it. "They don't tell you anything, you learn it through the seat
of your pants."

That few students seemed directed by strong moral convic-
tions, or had enough confidence to diverge from the standards of
those around them, was consistent with the peer-oriented, ap-
proval-seeking ways of their elders. That undergraduates more
and more turned off from politics, and that the Peace Corps
now attracted so few, mirrored the retreat of their parents into
purely private concerns. The I'll-get-mine philosophy of many
students was a product of a consumer-oriented society. It was
also a reflection of the changing fortunes of higher education,
as a quarter century of expansion came to an end.

II

Retrenchment's Angry Harvest

The malaise of the 1970s ran so deep that most students, preoccupied with their own troubles, gave little thought to the events that had produced it.

In the 1950s, as the Harvard classicist John Finley recalled, there had been "a wonderful optimism, everybody was going to get some place, and people were pleased with each other's successes." After 1957, the year the first Sputnik galvanized the science establishment and set off an unprecedented explosion of growth in academic research, student life began to change. University enrollments more than doubled between 1960 and 1970. The first glimmer of unrest appeared as undergraduates at universities that had been transformed overnight into vast factories of graduate research sensed the indifference of faculties and administrations to their concerns. As a result, many harbored a Luddite resentment against the machinery of education, an unrest that turned into anger as the universities continued paternalistically to interfere in students' personal and political activities. By the time the Vietnam war finally ignited a general rebellion, the protest movement that had begun at Berkeley and Michigan had already spread to other campuses. In the turmoil that followed, however, the original complaint of the students, that they were being oppressed by university authorities, was often lost sight of. It was only after the rebellion was over that students discovered to what degree their demands for more freedom had been granted. By then, the changes that were to lead to new tensions were being rapidly institutionalized.

The year 1970, which marked the tragic climax of the students' protest along with the close of a turbulent decade, saw as well the beginning of a widespread withdrawal throughout the society beyond the campuses. The new tensions that would plague students all through the 1970s were in large measure a reflection of the fortunes of middle-class suburbia and of the institutions it served. They were, in short, a manifestation of economic reality—the angry harvest of retrenchment.

Many schools had overextended themselves in the post-Sputnik era. The pressure for "relevancy" exerted by students had led universities to invest in expensive new departments and intensified the competition for teachers. Faculty salaries rose so rapidly as a consequence—outdistancing the wage increases in industry—that college budgets were strained. The cost of remedial programs for minority students was heavy. Yale, at the time it began admitting women and increasing the number of minority students, also added a hundred new professors to its faculty and opened an ambitious new graduate school. Brown had dipped into its endowment capital to meet the expenses of a burgeoning faculty and a complex of new science buildings. Many schools spent money as fast as they took it in.

When the expansionist boom petered out at the end of the 1960s, the universities had little left in reserve. Many were financially as well as emotionally spent; student disorders had forced heavy costs on them in added security, insurance and property damage, and had dampened the ardor of alumni contributors as well. The schools could no longer rely on Washington, on strapped state legislatures or the foundations for succor: amid the general economic slowdown, Federal grants declined; so did those from private foundations.

The real havoc had occurred when the slump in financial markets combined with the effects of uncontrolled inflation.

At four Ivy League universities—Brown, Dartmouth, Harvard and Princeton—operating expenditures between 1962 and 1972 went up by an average of 160 percent. By the mid-1970s, fuel charges alone had added a million dollars to annual university budgets. Between 1968 and 1976 at the University of Michigan, insurance costs escalated by more than 470 percent, and liability coverage, which protects the university and its staff from personal injury and damage claims, jumped 2,875 *percent* —from $104,000 to $3 million. The staggering utility costs impaired the ability of many schools to finance badly needed repair of old buildings and equipment; to defer such work meant a more painful reckoning to come. Meanwhile, during the decade that ended in 1977, the purchasing power of Yale's endowment had plunged by 40 percent, even as the school's operating costs had doubled; Harvard's huge nest egg, now worth about $1.4 billion, was badly cracked; at Brown, a never robust endowment was eroded by nearly 30 percent.

Even as Federal grants leveled off, the cost of complying with new Federal regulations in such fields as environmental protection and equal opportunity proliferated. The price tag to Harvard for administering five such government-ordered programs was running as high as $8 million a year. Efforts by the universities to reduce expenses often ran counter to the goals of affirmative action or ERA. When Columbia tried to save itself $100,000 by laying off thirty university maids, the maids responded with a suit charging sex discrimination; the layoff was reversed and Columbia ended up $50,000 out of pocket in legal fees.

Across the board, the effect on the leading schools—and on the quality of services they could offer—ranged from serious to devastating. "Probably no enterprise has been so hurt by today's combination of inflation and recession as has the private university," declared president Martin Meyerson of Penn, which faced a projected $7.6 million deficit in 1976–77 and was among those whose financial distress over the decade had raised questions about how long they might survive. Such schools as Berkeley, Chicago, Cornell, Stanford and Yale might not seem "to be on the ropes," as Harold Howe II, vice president for education and research at the Ford Foundation, put it. "But a good case can be made that they are heading in that direction with an acceleration that cannot be reversed without major new public and private initiatives within the next few years."

For much of the past decade Brown had been operating in the red, with deficits that forced severe cutbacks in faculty and scholarships; some observers foresaw the exhaustion of its unrestricted endowment by the mid-1980s. Yale's cumulative budget deficit reached nearly $17 million over ten years; in 1976 a loss of $6.6 million was the largest it had ever recorded in one year. Cornell experienced similar shortfalls. Columbia's fiscal troubles, said to be the worst in its 225-year history, frightened off a number of prospective applicants for the post of dean of the college, which remained vacant for months. Other elite schools, feeling the pinch, had to slash their faculties by five percent or more, as they watched teachers' salary increases slip further behind the inflation rate. The drop in Federal aid forced Dartmouth, among others, to freeze the enrollments in its Ph.D. programs.

The Cornell *Daily Sun* said it all one November day in 1975. Of five front-page stories, four concerned finances, with headlines reading: *Budget Calls for 9% Increase for Most Rooms; Aid Office Has No Money to Give New Transfers; Athletic Dept. Budget Faces Deficit;* and *University Makes Cut of $324,000 in Campus Life.*

Not even the old mainstay, the alumni, could be counted on for the same unstinting generosity as in the past. Though several universities, including Stanford and Princeton, concluded highly successful fund-raising drives in the 1970s, alumni donors had begun to appear grudging. The percentage of Harvard's alumni contributing to the college fund, for example, had dropped off since 1968, and other schools were complaining of reduced participation. A number of them waged mammoth capital-gift drives just to pay their bills—and fell embarrassingly short of the target. Alumni were deterred from contributing by the uncertainties of the economy, by philanthropic pressures closer to home and by anger over a range of past sins and upsetting new trends: student strikes, de-emphasis on ROTC, too many "liberals" on the faculty, and alumni sons getting short shrift from the admissions offices. Some disgruntled Princeton alumni even formed a group to propagandize against giving money to the college.

Educators on the elite campuses, at the end of the 1970s, could see little ahead but further austerity and new crises. According to one gallows joke, the only school with a chance of staying afloat was the University of the Seven Seas, a renovated ocean liner that was berthed somewhere along the California coast.

As Dartmouth's president, John Kemeny, put it, "The long-range problem is not one of our having to go out of business, but of having to compromise the quality of our education." Even at Harvard the dean of the faculty, Henry Rosovsky, warned that further reductions would threaten the quality of the college and its faculty. "There is a distinct danger," declared the 1979 prospectus for a new capital-gifts drive at Harvard, "that private institutions will no longer play the vital role in higher education that they have enjoyed in the past."

For all this, few of the students struggling with the burden of tuition and fees had sympathy to spare.

Between 1967 and 1978, Harvard's tuition, housing and medical fees per student rose 150 percent. By 1979 the combined fees per student at Harvard and Yale amounted to $7,500 or more a year. Tuition alone had leapfrogged ahead at a dizzying rate: in the Ivy League between 1971 and 1976 it rose an average of 50 percent, and in 1979 it exceeded $5,000 for the first time at a number of leading schools, including Brown and Princeton. In the 1950s the total annual living expenses for a student at such schools had amounted to less than $3,000; now the figure topped $8,000. With annual tuition, room and board escalating at a rate of six percent, one estimate had the total bill reaching $87,000 a year for a freshman in the class of A.D. 2000.

As inflation eroded the savings out of which most families paid their children's tuition fees, the burden fell increasingly on the students themselves. Many had to spend valuable time arranging loans, scrounging for the few available part-time jobs and calculating drastic new ways to cut expenses. "If you don't eat, you can bring your costs down," observed a Columbia dean, Patricia Geisler. "So some of them don't eat."

Many financial-aid recipients who had started working the commonly accepted ten hours a week on a part-time job soon found themselves dollar-short, and were spending from eighteen to twenty hours a week on two or more jobs. For Beth Johnson, a Brown senior laboring twenty hours a week as a baker's helper, baby-sitter and server in a snack shop, the regimen was all too typical: up at 4:30 A.M. three days a week for her job at the university bakery, and on alternate days racing at noon from her classes to the snack shop where she dispensed pizzas and ice cream. She averaged no more than five hours' sleep a night and squeezed in homework assignments at odd hours during the day. She worried as well about her ability to repay a $2,500 bank loan, and about the effects of the financial drain on her working parents. John Harris, a Harvard junior, cursed "the loans up to my head" and agonized for his schoolteacher mother and his father, a government employee, who were both contributing, more heavily each year, to Harris's education. Some students sought psychiatric help to assuage guilt feelings about their parents: the father who postponed retiring from a dreary job so as to help his son through Yale, the mother who started taking in laundry from neighbors.

Numbers of students accelerated their studies, graduating a year early to save on costs. Some hastened the process by earning summer-school credits at less expensive institutions; others transferred from prestigious institutions to state universities midway through their program. Increasingly, qualified students from financially pressed families did not even apply to elite schools because of the cost.

More than half of the students at leading colleages received some form of assistance, either in scholarships and direct loans from the college or through Federal grants or loans guaranteed by state or Federal government. By the late 1970s, with loans the fastest-growing component of financial aid, their borrowing at the eight Ivy League schools was estimated at a total of between $25 and $30 million. In the 1950s at one college, barely six percent of a class borrowed at all, and at graduation less than one percent reported debts of $2,500 or more. At that same college a quarter of a century later, as many as half the members of the class of 1981 were borrowing to finance their education, with debts averaging more than $5,000 by the time they left college. Those who went on to graduate school owed close to $10,000 when they were finished—a total indebtedness that, with interest, could top $16,000. A few educators predicted individual debts of twice that figure in the near future. If a student chose to marry someone else engaged in graduate work, as increasingly occurred, the combined debt might soar to between $50,000 and $100,000 before either spouse had earned a penny.

That prospect increased the pressure to bypass career choices that would benefit society as a whole in favor of more "marketable" study fields—such as engineering or business—that would ensure a quick disposal of one's college loan. The ablest students could be deterred from public service or pro bono legal work, and newly graduated M.D.'s would similarly shun public-health jobs in favor of lucrative specialties. For those who scorned thinking in "marketable" terms, the lack of such compensatory income led increasingly to defaults.

By 1978 close to 400,000 former students who had taken out Federally insured loans had either declared themselves bankrupt or simply refused to pay—a rate of default that exceeded 12 percent and included a substantial number of students who had attended elite universities. Some expressed anger over the rigid repayment schedules or bewilderment over the complex paperwork involved; many felt little remorse over their delinquency. At Berkeley, half of those who had taken out student loans were reported in default as of 1978; according to an HEW official, one student had defaulted on seven different loans and never paid a cent. Banks refusing to extend further loans to students compounded the dilemma of those in need of help.

Families who had once sent their children to the University of Pennsylvania now shunted them off to West Chester State College instead. "A lot of good students from upstate we never even see because they're so turned off by the thought of having to spend $7,000 or more a year," said Ted Lingenheld, admissions director at Penn. An official at Brown concurred: "They're selecting themselves out of here before they even apply." Concern over high costs, according to an internal survey, was the main reason why potential students who'd inquired about the University of Chicago later decided not to file an application. "It all just frightens people," concluded the admissions director at Harvard, where applications from the West and Midwest continued to decline appreciably.

"For less cost and sweat we could've been Phi Betes at a

state college and gone on to the grad schools of our choice," declared Louis DiGiovanni, a Yale student whose father worked as a cook in a New York City restaurant. The prospect of being shackled by huge debts was especially unappealing to minority students whose families' combined earnings might barely top $9,000, who had guilt pangs about being served more food in a day at college than their parents in the ghetto had to stretch over three days. Though proportionately the blacks received more aid, the number being granted outright scholarships declined as the retrenchment of the 1970s ran its course. Since blacks had a harder time securing good summer jobs, they were forced more often than whites to take out additional large loans if they were to stay in college.

But perhaps no group complained more of being unfairly penalized by the high costs of college than middle-income white students, sons and daughters of relatively debt-free families whose earnings, in the $15,000 to $30,000 range, were no longer enough to carry the full costs of their studies at Yale or Stanford but were frequently enough to disqualify them from receiving financial aid. "If you're middle-income you don't qualify for anything," fumed a woman senior at Brown. "You have to fight to get a loan, fight to get any financial aid. You can be just five hundred dollars over the limit, and they'll say no."

By the latter part of the decade, the proportion of middle-income students accepting offers of admission from some prestigious schools had dropped anywhere from 10 to 20 percent below the average. Significantly, the lowest proportion of acceptances—51 percent—came from those applicants whose parents were expected to contribute a heavy share of the costs of tuition and board.

All of this produced alarming visions of great universities eventually polarized between the rich and the poor. An editorial in the *Daily Princetonian* warned of "a return to the stereotyped one-class Princeton of the rich." The chief admissions officer of another university declared: "We can't afford to lose that predominant middle group that is the great connector between the other two." It was of equal concern that those high-scoring students from middle-income families had long comprised the primary market of the elite schools. As inflation continued, and increasing numbers of families moved into the $20,000 income range, the problem could worsen. "Our schools have now gotten themselves into a corner from which we cannot easily escape," said Thomas O'Brien, Harvard's financial vice president. "Unless schools are very careful, they will not only run the danger of pricing themselves out of the market, they will price themselves out of the range of an upper-middle-income family's ability to pay under any but the most exceptional circumstances."

The dwindling enrollment of middle-income students forced universities such as Harvard, Stanford and Michigan to devise more liberal loan programs for them, while Congress in 1978 approved plans to extend Federal grants to students whose families earned up to $25,000 a year. (The old income ceiling had been $15,000.) Other schemes under consideration included authorizing tuition tax credits to ease the burden on parents and allotting more than a billion dollars in direct aid to the universities, to be allocated as they saw fit. Some colleges considered awarding larger amounts of aid solely for academic merit; at the same time, more high school seniors than ever applied for advance standing at college as a way of eliminating an expensive semester or two from their education. The efforts came none too soon to head off the prospect of a generation of indentured students, many of whom had little hope or intention of repaying their creditors on time.

Inevitably, the stringent economizing that most colleges had forced upon them in the 1970s hastened a decline in the quality of campus life. Few universities were able to avoid scarring cuts in their faculties, administrative staffs and student services. Though tenured professors remained largely untouched, the casualties often included precisely those junior faculty members and counselors who had the closest ties to students.

There was now a fear that a lot of the things students had successfully fought for in the 1960s—more varied curricula, better student services, a greater role for minorities—would be squeezed out by financial considerations. There was also anger and disbelief that institutions with a legacy of wealth should have to decree cutbacks and ever-increasing fees to make ends meet.

At Brown, a proposal to eliminate between fifty and seventy-five of the university's five hundred faculty positions was one of the sparks that ignited the student strike in 1975. A year later, Cornell was projecting more than 160 faculty departures through layoffs and attrition; Penn anticipated the loss of sixty arts-and-sciences faculty members, most of them part-time instructors and teaching assistants. Dartmouth had to abort a popular experimental social program that regularly brought professors and students together over supper in the dining halls. University cost-cutters increasingly nicked students with new "user" fees, covering everything from check-cashing to the use of campus game rooms. Cornell even considered reducing the capacity of beer containers at the university tavern.

Of all the services offered students, none was more vital than the campus library, and even there the economic toll was visible. "The condition of the books is frightening," reported the director of Harvard's undergraduate library, where the cost of rebinding had risen so steeply that the restoration of damaged books appeared to be in jeopardy. With book prices in the 1970s rising by as much as 18 percent annually, the purchasing power of libraries was seriously eroded: it now took at least four times as much money to acquire the same number of new U. S. publications as in 1960. Libraries were frequently understaffed, unable to replace missing books or to subscribe to new periodicals. The University of Chicago's Regenstein Library, one of the world's great academic collections, became (in the words of an internal university report) "a living example of hand-to-mouth operations." Joel Silbey, a professor at Cornell, warned: "A situation beautifully designed to accommodate undergraduates is breaking down because of crowding and budget cuts. Our whole library system could collapse or at least change drastically, affecting the education of our students."

Efforts to economize backfired at times, temporarily worsening the living conditions on campus.

In late 1977 a deficit-ridden Yale refused to meet the salary demands of its blue-collar employees, who proceeded to go on strike, shutting down the campus dining halls and other services. Students who were paying nearly $8,000 a year for the privilege of matriculating at Yale were forced to empty their own trash, clean up bathrooms and look for meals on their own. Hours at the library and gymnasium were curtailed. Some students got into fist fights with the picketing workers; others laid the blame on the university.

For some time, students had stoically accepted the spiraling costs or invented ploys for offsetting them—a Stanford group invested in a thoroughbred race horse which they named "Our Tuition"—but by the middle of the decade, patience had worn thin. "I'm one who expects to be forced out of Cornell or else into fantastic debt," an irate senior wrote to the student paper. Dartmouth undergraduates called on the college to chop off the administrative "deadwood," and student leaders at Penn made similar demands. With mounting frequency the frustration began spilling over into confrontations that raised the ghost of the 1960s.

Students at Rutgers, Northwestern and the University of Rochester rallied against tuition increases. Thousands of state university students from New York and New Jersey marched on state capitols, where there were scuffles with police, over the issue of cutbacks in financial aid. Undergraduates at Princeton gathered to hector the trustees as they met on campus to confirm a $625 raise in tuition and fees. In 1975–76, protests erupted as well at Penn, Chicago and Cornell. "Cut the budget, not our throats!" read one placard at Penn. Early in 1978, when Penn's administration announced a number of budget cutbacks in athletic and theatre programs, outraged students marched again—some 1,200 of them. They occupied the administration building for three and a half days, during which tense negotiations with Penn officials were punctuated by a bomb threat and the chanting of obscene slogans. In another campus building, black students supporting the demonstration staged their own sit-in and added a set of new demands. The final settlement restored some of the endangered programs (though the university's hockey team was disbanded) and called for a student representative to sit on the board of trustees on a trial basis. According to a Penn spokesman, Theodore Driesch,

"The pressures on the administration haven't been this serious in my ten years here."

More students than ever before now sat on university committees, but they had only limited power to halt the firing of a popular young assistant professor or the promotion of some reclusive savant with tenure. Where students enjoyed a modicum of fiscal control, it could prove short-lived: at Cornell the student–faculty senate that emerged at the end of the 1960s to become custodian of a $20-million budget was abolished by the university's trustees in 1977. As layoffs among recently hired black or women faculty members jeopardized the gains of earlier years, students began to question whether university administrations were sincerely committed to equality of treatment for minorities.

Few students advocated the inmates' taking over the asylum, but many remained frustrated at having so little say in decisions affecting their welfare. And notwithstanding the enormous changes that had been brought about by the generation preceding them, the more thoughtful students now seemed curiously forlorn. Roberta Campbell, an assistant dean at Columbia, couldn't believe she was actually mourning for the antic days of water fights and the exuberance of protest demonstrations. In vain she searched the dormitories for a blithe spirit. Few students seemed to savor the once loose, sweet time of undergraduatehood. "They're twenty-one going on sixty," concluded a University of Chicago chaplain. "They've forgotten how to laugh."

"Everything we came to admire, from men to institutions, died or fell apart just as we recognized them," mused Elisa Cabot, a 21-year-old junior at the University of Pennsylvania. "We'd begun to respect the presidency just as Kennedy was murdered, we were giving our hearts to civil rights when King was shot down. Government and legal institutions had begun to touch our consciousness, our loyalty—then, Vietnam and Watergate. What's left to believe in other than Self?" In the words of Jean Benefield, a Yale divinity student, "All we see is the futility of it all. We can't change anything."

In the 1960s, students had been able to channel their dissatisfaction against identifiable villains: Bull Connor, Lyndon Johnson, General Hershey. But the issues of the 1970s—energy, world hunger, inflation, pollution—offered few such targets for blame. Thus, a lot of students lapsed into what Stanford's president, Richard Lyman, called "an unearned cynicism." What some observers mistook for apathy was in fact a fear of commitment, of risking further disillusionment, that drove some students to demand protection against a future about which they had little reason to be sanguine. "Instead of joining others for change," concluded a prominent Stanford sociologist, "this generation is giving up and saying, 'How am I going to survive?' "

Moral issues were not entirely forgotten. In the spring of 1978, sit-ins and torchlight rallies at several leading universities protested the policy of maintaining investments in South Africa, the home of apartheid. At Harvard the issue was responsible for the largest student demonstration since 1970. The university's president had to be rescued from a mob of screaming protesters. "A sense of fear born of past memories of student activism is growing," declared an editorial in the undergraduate daily *Crimson*. "Harvard is both afraid of and unwilling to listen to its own no-longer-docile students."

Alfred Bowker, chancellor of the University of California at Berkeley, recalling to a visitor how the Vietnam war had finally catalyzed the students' deeper discontent into open revolt, likewise warned of tensions and resentments simmering beneath the surface. "It's getting close to what I would have guessed the emotional climate was like in '68," said Glen Hopkins, a senior at Columbia.

In 1930, more than a thousand students had had to withdraw from the University of Michigan because of insolvency. Although the financial stress of the late 1970s hadn't reached such proportions, educators agreed that not since the Great Depression had students been so grimly conscious of how much it cost to attend college. As the 1980s loomed, one educator warned, "A basic uneasiness on campus could easily be converted to activism if their very legitimate concerns are not addressed. It will surely take far less to radicalize our young today than at the time of the Great Depression."

Resentful students were already mobilizing, often more resourcefully than the antiwar activists of the 1960s. They formed research and lobbying groups, swung reciprocal arrangements with campus employees, hired lawyers, circulated petitions, plotted tuition strikes and the picketing of trustees' business headquarters. This time, moreover, it would not be only or primarily the children of the comfortable upper class who revolted in large numbers. "Black students will act," said a black professor at the University of Pennsylvania, "and you're going to see the kind of confrontation we saw in the 1960s, only much uglier." A dean at one Ivy League college warned: "The anger and frustration is all just beneath the surface. If the wrong events transpire, it could all come rushing out again."

The danger was that the elite schools, as they entered the decade of the 1980s, would be forced to devote more energies to their own survival than to the spread of unrest among their students. Though the outcome remained in doubt, it was clear at the end of the decade that the angry harvest of retrenchment was on its way.

12

A Way Out of the Trap

The beginning of the end for a number of select private institutions came on a February day in 1981.

That morning Columbia announced yet another five-hundred-dollar increase in tuition for the coming fall. On the stroke of noon a siren began wailing from the roof of Baker Library and moments later James Archer, a 21-year-old Columbia prelaw student and newly elected head of the national Save the Middleclass Student movement (SMS), led more than two thousand angry undergraduates out of their classrooms to protest the hike. Within hours the Columbia administration was reeling under a massive tuition boycott; SMS announced that students would refuse to pay any further bills and would place all tuition funds in escrow, pending the outcome of the protest.

Word of the action at Columbia reached upstate Cornell that afternoon, and for the fifth time in as many years, hundreds of restive black students began milling in front of the administration building. This time, several thousand sullen whites joined them. The show of force persuaded Cornell officials to postpone their own impending announcement of a further tuition increase and to suspend classes indefinitely. The news hit Brown University just as students there were being advised that tuition and boarding fees would go up by another ten percent in the fall. In a replay of the 1975 strike, a thousand-strong alliance of blacks and whites walked out of classes; at the same time, Brown's entire staff of service employees left their jobs in support of the students. Similar actions followed at the universities of Pennsylvania and Chicago, where students and workers had forged close ties and recently established joint bargaining units.

At Michigan, Harvard, Yale and Berkeley, where SMS maintained strong undergraduate chapters, university operations ground to a halt as protest swept the campuses. Sporadic violence kept local police on edge; at Ann Arbor, state troopers waited on alert outside the university gates. A bursar was roughed up at one school, the university treasurer assaulted in his office at another. Smoke bombs forced the evacuation of the budget staff from Sproul Hall at Berkeley, and several staffers were briefly hospitalized.

Alarmed officials at some of the institutions debated whether to withdraw their plans for upcoming tuition hikes; but word of the plans had already leaked out, and the students' reaction could not be forestalled. Two other national groups, the Coalition of Private University Students (COPUS) and the Student Union Movement of America (SUMMA), mobilized for action. Thousands of SUMMA-organized students threw up picket lines around the homes of university presidents and the company offices of prominent trustees. COPUS, with members from Columbia, Princeton, Stanford, Penn and Yale, dispatched busloads of protesters to Washington to lobby against the hikes and demand more government aid. The protesters marched on the White House, thronged Congressional offices on Capitol Hill and held a torchlight rally on the steps of the Lincoln Memorial.

While SMS activists neutralized the campuses, SUMMA leaders forced university officials to meet with them to renegotiate such issues as tuition, financial aid, housing fees and rollbacks in student services. There were demands for effective tax relief for parents of middle-income students and for an extension of the payback time for students who'd borrowed heavily to finance their education. Telegrams of support from student groups in Italy, France and West Germany poured into SMS and SUMMA headquarters. Lawyers for COPUS, meanwhile, prepared a series of multi-million-dollar test suits against several leading schools, charging them with discriminatory financial aid policies and with having deprived students of their civil right to participate in budgetary decisions affecting their welfare.

The crisis confronted the universities with a dismal Hobson's choice. A number of financially shaky ones, faced with the prospect of continued turmoil or bankruptcy, collapsed under the pressure and announced that they would not reopen in the fall. Others, desperate to survive even as wards of the government, quietly prepared for the inevitable transfer from independent to public status.

As of 1979, none of this had happened—yet. But it is not an unthinkable scenario. SUMMA might be only a writer's invention, but COPUS already existed and it was probably but a matter of time before students organized something like SMS. "We'll go through a terrible survival crisis and many institutions won't make it," was the prediction of William McGill, president of Columbia University, when I talked with him during my visit to that campus. After months of interviewing educators and students across the country, it is my own conviction that things will worsen before they improve. Declining enrollments may mean that fewer students will have to vie with one another for admission to professional schools, but the glut in the key professions implies that law and medical schools will be increasingly selective, and competition to enter them more intense than ever. A siege mentality prevails as the colleges anticipate further budget-paring and cutbacks in programs.

When I closed my notebook for the last time, I understood all too well what the Harvard sociologist David Riesman had meant when he described the mood on the campuses as one of "desperate anxiety." Before I began the more than six hundred interviews that are the basis of this book, I couldn't have envisioned such a mood. Superficially, the gamboling of frisbee players, the rites of the fall football season, the carillons chiming vespers, suggested that nothing had changed very much. But a friend had told me of his daughter's ordeal at Yale as two of her roommates succumbed to mental breakdowns. The mother of a freshwoman at Stanford had told me of her daughter's being assaulted and raped while she sunbathed in the campus foothills. And in my opening interview with an educator—Henry Coleman, dean of students at Columbia—I heard of the pressures that had destroyed the old tranquillity. "I've told my wife," Coleman said, "that I hope our kids *won't* be doctors or lawyers."

The students themselves regarded me warily at first—as one more outsider come to examine the psychology of the inmates. I remember one senior at the University of Chicago sitting in icy silence, defying my every effort to draw her out. Yet little by little, they would open up, revealing in disjointed fragments their pain and confusion. From an hour with student leaders at the University of Michigan, it became apparent that the lack of decent housing overrode nearly every other concern on that campus. At Yale, dinner with four undergraduates in their off-campus apartment had been strangely muted until one of them blurted out that it had been exactly a year before that their former roommate, Gary Stein, had gone off to visit his girlfriend and never come back.

The shocks came in cumulative bursts of candor from the students—in my dawning realization that so many of them viewed their lives and selves with contempt, that so few of them found their college experience enriching or pleasurable. They recognized the cheating around them, and looked the other way. They sensed the shallowness of their careerist aims, and plunged blindly ahead. A black senior explained how he hated Harvard for serving the attitudes of the elite, yet forced himself to adapt in order to win his "ticket to security." A senior at Yale confided that he had decided to become a labor lawyer so he could learn "to use the law to *my* advantage." I listened with dismay to young careerists expressing their scorn for liberal arts as an upper-class luxury: the prebusiness student at the University of Pennsylvania who said, "If I'd been born with a silver spoon in my mouth, then I could sit back and enjoy developing my intellect." And, though I knew that the old nostalgia for Alma Mater was long gone, I found it still appalling that so many students viewed themselves as mere transients with no loyalties to their college.

What shocked me most, however, was the numbness, emotional as well as moral, that I encountered everywhere. I remember too well the conclusion of Fred Wall, president of the class of '76 at Dartmouth—that "more and more students don't react to situations and, more terrifying, don't react to people." And I had to concur with the judgment of Eric Holtzman, a professor at Columbia: "The sense of freedom to explore, to be an exuberant learner, is greatly restrained. You feel if you make a mistake, you're done for."

It was this tight-rope syndrome, more than anything, that marked the 1970s generation at the elite schools from their predecessors. Other generations had been subjected to pressures, but none had seemed so daunted by them or begun agonizing over them so early in their lives. Freshmen entered college with their entire four-year study program already drawn up; they were already wrestling with decisions over whether to establish friendships, seek out monagamous relationships or get married. The earlier they began trying to order their future, the more time there was to let the obstacles and fears build up in their minds. Many of them, raised indulgently in a cotton-candy world, were unprepared to cope with the pressures. Never having tasted defeat in their childhoods, they panicked at the thought of having to face it now.

To report that students at our leading universities have lost their moral and cultural bearings in such large numbers is to admit to disgrace. It may be that the universities cannot be blamed for the failings of parents and of the society as a whole; but neither can they be allowed to fall back on such an exculpation. It is time for them to reassert their role in upholding cultural values—to declare that they are *not* in the business of purveying knowledge as a salable commodity. Nor is it any more acceptable that so many undergraduates must contend, quite aside from academic pressure, with crowded and substandard housing, the threat of crime and the erosion of simple courtesy.

As a reporter, I do not pretend to offer in detail a prescription for what can or ought to be done by way of reform. But I venture to suggest the following:

❰ COMMITTED TEACHING should be rewarded as a matter of policy. Annual stipends and public recognition should single out those faculty members whom their students recognize as caring and receptive, who communicate values of their own and who are willing, as Bartlett Giamatti, the newly installed president of Yale, has urged, "to stand up and speak out"—recognizing, as Giamatti himself has put it, that "there's too damn much ambiguity."

❰ INEQUITIES IN GRADING should be reduced, and inflated grades made a punishable offense.

❰ THE CORE CURRICULUM should be restored to reduce the confusion and pressure over choice of studies. This is already happening at Harvard, where educational requirements had grown flabby, and a bloated course catalog included 2,600 separate listings. The need is as great elsewhere: for example, at Yale, where in 1975 more than 40 percent of the graduating seniors had not taken a full-year course in science or mathematics, and more than 20 percent had not taken a basic course in English literature.

❨ FORTHRIGHT ACTION must be taken to defuse the racial tensions that are poisoning college life. Regular meetings between black and white student leaders, attended by deans and faculty representatives, can do something to forestall the growing polarization. More can be done by university administrations to discipline blatantly racist conduct. Clubs and fraternities that systematically exclude minorities are an anachronism that should be ended; and the same applies to exclusively black residential houses and sports teams.

❨ THE OPTION of living in single-sex dormitories should be available to students who prefer not to be subjected to the pressures of co-residency. More should be done to curb the practice of undergraduates who disrupt the lives of their roommates by inviting sexual partners to become permanent lodgers in dormitory rooms.

❨ A SERIOUS EFFORT should be made to set up alternate career routes for those rejected by schools of medicine, law and business—many of whom now tend to be so embittered by a sense of wasted effort as to have become, in the words of one college president, "a profoundly dangerous force in society." Special degree programs in public policy, in museum and foundation management, in educational television and in primary health care—to suggest a few examples—should siphon off some of the overflow and ease the pressure of competition.

Nevertheless, the pressure will be there for so long as the present unrealistic attitude toward an elite college education remains unchanged.

We encourage our children to enter college as though it were at once a passport to maturity and an escalator to prestige, security and a high income. We sanction its role as grooming stables for the professions, whereas what we should expect above all is to have our children's minds set afire with the excitement of learning. What we must do now is to reassess our attitudes and temper our expectations. It must be understood that four years at a leading college cannot be expected to guarantee social success, emotional fulfillment, permanently expanded cultural horizon *and* entry into a top professional school, all at once. We are entitled to expect good teachers, sympathetic advisers and a demonstrable concern for the students that is equal to the concern over endowments and scholarly research.

As for the students themselves, it is time to slow down the headlong rush toward professional success and consider the alternatives. The student who, fresh out of college, builds a log cabin in the Maine woods or rafts down the Amazon; the one who drops out for a year, not to travel and get his head together, but to help in a community day-care center or work as a volunteer in a hospital—has not quite become extinct but is rare enough to seem an anomaly in a generation that has so largely adopted a bookkeeper's approach to achievement, measuring it in board scores, grade points and expectable income. Far too many students in the 1970s have become so obsessed with their entitlements, along with the determination to come out first, that the notion of responsibility seems to have been lost sight of almost entirely.

On campus after campus, I listened to educators who envisaged a millennium in which the professions were wholly dominated by such attitudes—by businessmen whose preoccupation with the bottom line has obliterated all social concern, by doctors who have lost the ability to diagnose along with any intuitive feel for the patient as a whole person, by lawyers who have lost sight of every goal other than the maximizing of corporate profits. Their vision of the future was, in short, a leadership without a soul presiding over a technological system without a conscience.

Too harsh a prediction? Perhaps. But, as Roderic Park, the provost of the University of California at Berkeley, reminds us, "Nazi Germany was filled with exquisitely trained people."

There was, in fact, a schizoid quality about many of these students: so cynical, yet so vulnerable; yearning for empathy, yet desperately competitive; ambitious, yet lacking in true confidence. They had amassed all the knowledge of a computer, but lacked ability to grapple with creative ideas—an army of one-dimensional achievers with their clipboards and crisp sense of priorities. Without bold dreams or even the sustaining belief that things would turn out all right in the end, they had neither the idealism nor the élan of previous college generations. They were, in the end, victims of our expectations as parents—trapped between the possibility of intellectual excitement and the pressure to justify the draining financial investment we have made in educating them.

Of those who held out against that pressure, I remember a Harvard junior, Joe Knowles, who was one of the happier students I met, who had made his peace with the values he saw around him but elected to "go my own way." A government major with a B average, he had dismissed the notion of joining the rush for law school, and had found fulfillment working in his spare time for a Boston politician and for a campus organization that served the poor of the area. Whether the future belongs to Joe Knowles and others like him, I cannot say. But his independent spirit points to one way out of the trap. Indeed, there may be no other.

Bibliography

American Council on Education. *The Labor Market for College Graduates.* Washington, D. C., June 1975.

"Analysis of Trends in Drug Use Behavior at Five American Universities," *Journal of School Health,* September 1974.

Becker, Howard S., Blanche Geer, Anselm L. Strauss, and Everett Hughes. *Boys in White: Student Culture in Medical School.* Chicago: University of Chicago Press, 1961.

Becker, Howard S., Blanche Geer, and Everett C. Hughes. *Making the Grade: The Academic Side of College Life.* New York: John Wiley & Sons, 1968.

Belknap, Robert L., and Richard Kuhns. *Tradition and Innovation: General Education and the Reintegration of the University.* New York: Columbia University Press, 1977.

Berman, Susan. *The Underground Guide to the College of Your Choice.* New York: New American Library, 1971.

Bird, Caroline. *The Case Against College.* New York: David McKay, 1975.

Bok, Derek C. "Can Ethics Be Taught?" *Change,* October 1976.

———. *The President's Report.* Cambridge: Harvard University Press, 1974, 1975, 1976, 1977, 1978.

Bok, Sissela. *Lying: Moral Choice in Public and Private Life.* New York: Pantheon Books, 1978.

Bowers, William J. *Student Dishonesty and Its Control in College.* New York: Columbia University, Bureau of Applied Social Research, 1964.

Brenner, Steven, and Earl Molander. "Is the Ethics of Business Changing?" *Harvard Business Review,* January–February 1977.

Brickman, William. "Ethics, Examinations & Experiments," *Intellect,* October 1974.

Chamber of Commerce of the United States. *White Collar Crime.* Washington, D. C., 1974.

Cohen, Peter. *The Gospel According to the Harvard Business School.* Penguin Books, New York–Baltimore, 1974.

Consortium on Financing Higher Education. *Enrolling the Class of 1978: An Analysis of the 1974 Student Market at Twenty-Three Private Institutions.* Hanover, New Hampshire, September 1975.

Cooper, Irving S. *The Victim Is Always the Same.* New York: Harper & Row, 1973.

Cornell University. *Report of the Trustee Ad Hoc Committee on the Status of Minorities.* Ithaca, New York, October 1975.

————. *Report of the Special Trustee Committee on Campus Unrest at Cornell.* Ithaca, New York, September 1969.

Dawson, Charles F., and Ralph Edwards. "Competition Among Pre-Medical Students," *Columbia College Pre-Med*, Volume III (Summer 1964).

"Deceptiveness in Competition," *Journal of Moral Education*, Volume 3, pp. 159–165 (February 1974).

"Drugs & Sex: Scene of Ambivalence," *Journal of American College Health Association*, Vol. 21, pp. 438–488 (June 1973).

"Ethics & Morality in American Business & Government," *Business Education Forum*, Volume 28, pp. 40–42 (April 1974).

Federal Bureau of Investigation. *Crime in the U.S. 1975* (Uniform Crime Reports).

Fisher, Francis D. *One Thousand Men of Harvard: The Harvard College Class of 1971 Five Years Later.* Cambridge, Mass.: Harvard University, 1976.

————. *Report on the Class of 1976.* Office of Career Services. Cambridge, Mass.: Harvard University, 1977.

Fiske, Edward. "Teaching Morality in Schools," *New York Times*, May 4, 1975.

Gallagher, Buell. *Campus in Crisis.* New York: Harper & Row, 1969.

Gilbert Youth Research Survey. *Youth, 1974.* New York: Research Services, Institute of Life Insurance.

Gordon, Ernest. *Meet Me at the Door.* New York: Harper & Row, 1969.

Guzzardi, Walter, Jr. *The Young Executives.* New York: Mentor Executive Library, 1965.

Hackman, Judith, and John Hoskins. *Patterns of Successful Performance in Yale College.* New Haven: Yale University, August 1975.

Hardwick, Elizabeth. "Domestic Manners," *Daedalus*, Winter 1978.

Harp, John, and Philip Taietz. "Academic Integrity & Social Structure: A Study of Cheating Among College Students," *Social Problems*, Spring 1966.

Hechinger, Fred and Grace. *Growing Up in America.* New York: McGraw–Hill, 1975.

Hendin, Herbert. "Student Suicide: Death as a Life Style," *Journal of Nervous and Mental Diseases*, March 1975.

Hettlinger, Richard. *Sex Isn't That Simple: The New Sexuality on Campus.* New York: Seabury Press, 1974.

Hoffer, William. "What's Being Done About Campus Suicide," *College Management*, April 1972.

Horner, Matina. "Changes Ahead in Higher Education," *Radcliffe Quarterly*, March 1978.

Kaske, Neal, and Donald Thompson. *A Report on the Moffitt Undergraduate Library Book Theft Study.* Berkeley: University of California, 1975.

Lamb, Robert. "Professional Schools: Cram Courses in Tension and Trauma," *New York Times Magazine*, November 20, 1977.

Lasch, Christopher. "The Narcissist Society," *New York Review of Books*, September 30, 1976.

LeBoutillier, John. *Harvard Hates America.* South Bend, Indiana: Gateway Editions Ltd., 1978.

Lipset, Seymour, and David Riesman. *Education and Politics at Harvard.* New York: McGraw–Hill, 1975.

McCarthy, Abigail. "Walker Makes the Road: College Students," *Commonweal,* September 27, 1974.

Maccoby, Michael. *The Gamesman.* New York: Simon & Schuster, 1976.

Margolis, Richard J. "Steps Toward Maturity," *Change,* January 1976.

Munter, Preston K. *Depression and Suicide in College Students.* Boston, Mass.: Harvard University Health Services, 1975.

Murphy, William, and J. D. R. Bruckner, eds. *The Idea of the University of Chicago.* Chicago: University of Chicago Press, 1976.

Newman, John Henry Cardinal. *The Idea of a University.* Westminster, Md.: Christian Classics Inc., 1973.

"Patterns of College Student Drug Use," *Psychological Reports,* Volume 33, pp. 76–86 (August 1973).

Paying for College: Financing Education at Nine Private Institutions. Hanover, New Hampshire: The University Press of New England, 1974.

Pendleton, J. D. "Education for Honesty?" *Today's Education,* March 1975.

Pusey, Nathan M. *American Higher Education 1945–1970.* Cambridge: Harvard University Press, 1978.

"Research, Fear and the Student Cheater," *Change,* Volume 6, pp. 47–48 (August 1974).

Riesman, David. *The Lonely Crowd.* New Haven: Yale University Press, 1973.

Royster, Vermont. "The Public Morality," *American Scholar,* Spring 1974.

Simmons, Adele. "The Deceptive Calm on Today's Campuses," *University: A Princeton Quarterly,* Fall 1974.

Simon, Sidney. "Grades Must Go," *Changing Education,* Spring 1970.

Sizer, Nancy F. and Theodore R. *Moral Education.* Cambridge: Harvard University Press, 1973. (Five Lectures by James M. Gustafson, Richard S. Peters, Lawrence Kohlberg, Bruno Bettelheim and Kenneth Keniston.)

Stavisky, Leonard Price. "Term Paper Mills, Academic Plagiarism and State Regulation," *Political Science Quarterly,* September 1973.

"Student Work Loads," *Higher Education,* Volume 2, pp. 447–460 (November 1973).

Talbot, Nathan B. *Raising Children in Modern America.* Boston: Little, Brown, 1976.

"Test Anxiety and Cheating on College Exams," *Psychological Reports,* Volume 32, pp. 149–150.

Toffler, Alvin. *Future Shock.* New York: Random House, 1970.

Turow, Scott. *One L, Life in the First Year at Harvard Law School.* New York: G. P. Putnam's Sons, 1977.

"University Student Attitudes & Behavior Toward Drugs," *Journal of College Student Personnel,* Volume 13, pp. 236–237 (May 1973).

Watts, William, and Lloyd Free, eds. *State of the Nation.* New York: Potomac Associates, Universe Books, 1973.

"Why Do Students Cheat?" *American Observer,* March 8, 1971.

"Why Johnny Can't Flunk: Term-Paper Companies," *Esquire,* April 1973.

Wise, Helen D. *What Do We Tell the Children? Watergate and the Future of Our Country.* New York: George Braziller, 1974.

Wright, John C., and Richard Kelly. "Cheating: Student/Faculty Views & Responsibilities," *Improving College & University Teaching*, Winter 1974.

Yale Health Service. *Rape and the Yale Student.* New Haven, 1976.

Yankelovitch, Daniel. *The New Morality: A Profile of American Youth in the '70's.* New York: McGraw–Hill, 1974.

Index

DATE DUE